Vancouver Cooks

with Caren McSherry

Oct '94
Caren McSherry

Published by

Great Culinary Adventures Inc.

1856 Pandora Street,

Vancouver, B.C. V5L 1M5

Tel:(604) 255-5119 Fax: (604) 253-1331

Published in 1994 in Vancouver, British Columbia, Canada
  by **Great Culinary Adventures Inc.,**
  1856 Pandora Street, Vancouver,
  British Columbia, Canada
  Tel: (604) 255-5119, Fax: (604) 253-1331

Canadian Cataloguing in Publication Data
McSherry, Caren 1952-
  Vancouver Cooks with Caren McSherry

Includes index.
ISBN 0-9698838-0-3
1. Cookery. I. Title
TX714.M37 1994   641.5   C94-910843-X

DESIGN LAYOUT & PRODUCTION: Robyn Huth Design Co.
PHOTOGRAPHY: Greg Athans
AUTHOR PHOTOGRAPH: Jane Weitzel
EDITED BY: Linda Brandt/ElizabethWilson
FOOD STYLIST: Tina Salter

Color separated by LithoTech Canada Ltd.
Printed and bound in Vancouver by Printcraft of B.C. Limited and
Coast Trade Bindery Ltd.

10 9 8 7 6 5 4 3 2

For my mother,

Clara McSherry

Who taught me to never give up

and reach for the stars.

Thank you for always being there

and believing anything is possible.

Acknowledgements

In November, 1978 I began my very first cooking class to a sold-out audience of 6. With that, the development of my career and lifetime passion for good food also began. My cooking school program now bursts with 30 different classes each semester to sell-out attendance of 35 enthusiastic students. I owe a special thank you to these devoted patrons who have badgered me into this great adventure, my first cookbook, a complete compendium of Caren's Cooking School favorite recipes.

It is not without help, encouragement and special friends that one is able to even begin the publication of a book. I want to recognize all of those very special people who have cheered, encouraged, and supported me on this project. My thank yous are truly sincere, as without all of these people dedicating their talents and energies, *Vancouver Cooks with Caren McSherry* would never have been.

I met Linda Brandt at a food professionals conference and have her to thank for motivating me to realize my long term goal and write this cookbook.

Elizabeth Wilson, co-editor, your incredible knowledge of food & wine certainly contributed to the wealth of this book.

Robyn Huth, the book art director who worked tirelessly to meet many harrowing deadlines; thank you so much for burning the midnight oil during the last week, ensuring all the details were perfect. You are a terrific person.

Tina Salter, for your wonderful food styling, patience and perfectionism;

Cindy Burridge, Doreen Corday, Michelle Corday, Ruth Grierson, Donna Halkier, Patrick Hartney, Pauline Jones, Lana Quinn, John Ward, Murray Wooldridge: thank you for tirelessly testing all of the recipes to iron out all the kinks;

Ann Vallee for your terrific ability to organize, promote, glossarize; thank you for your persistently optimistic attitude, I appreciate you being there for all the hours of the day and night.

Rhonda May, editor and publisher, *CityFood* Magazine, thank you for your support, kind words and friendship; Kerry Sear, friend and executive chef at the Four Seasons Hotel in Seattle, for your fabulous Calamari recipe; Renee Blackstone, Hugh Carpenter, and Michel Jacob for your very encouraging words. Thank you so much; Doreen Corday, Donna Halkier and Tina Salter for the loan of your very beautiful dishes in the photo shoot; and Artistic Marble for the loan and use of the granite and marble slabs in our photos.

To my dear friend Cindy Burridge who is not only my right arm at the cooking school but also the backbone of my business organization; thank you for all your extra efforts during the last frenzied month. You are fabulous.

Thank you to my pillars of support, my best friends, who have stood tirelessly listening and encouraging: three cheers to my wonderful friends, Diane and Susan.

Last and most important to my family, my husband José Valagao, my daughter Christina and son Jason who showed unbelievable patience and love while I sat in the basement pounding away on my computer. Thank you José for sharing your wine knowledge and making the selections for each recipe and helping to perfect the flavors. Thank you for believing in me and encouraging me with this project. You have filled me with inspiration and I love you for it!

 able of Contents

Introduction   6

Glossary   8

Starters   14

Bread, Pizza and Pasta   55

Entrees   86

Desserts   122

Metric Equivalents   152

Index   153

About the Author   158

Order Form   159

Introduction

At the CityFood *Magazine offices we get a stack of new cookbooks every week for review purposes and looking at them always begs the question: "Does the world need another cookbook?" I once calculated that if I attempted 3 recipes a day until every book in our library was tested I would, at the end of the project be something like 1,537 years old. So the answer to the question is no, not at all and yes, absolutely! It depends on the cookbook. Or more to the point, it depends on who wrote it.*

What we do not need is another book cooked up by an initiate of the secret society of chefs "first debone an entire duck being careful to keep the carcass in its original shape." Nor do we need another superwoman marathon manual "place the free-range eggs gathered fresh this morning from the hen house you keep at the back of your estate into the antique egg cups you found on your last roadster trip through the Poconos and surround with the macraméd doilies you have crocheted especially for the occasion." And what we definitely do not need is any more books where the author would have us holding out our fingers in the sign of the cross before a chocolate chip cookie "this is a chocolate fudge brownie with no chocolate, no sugar, no butter" — no point. These sorts of books make you feel tired, inadequate, and unloved. I say lets go back to wood-burning stoves and use these tomes for fuel.

What we do need is more books that are unpretentious, helpful and inspiring. Which is why Vancouver Cooks with Caren McSherry *is a book to keep on hand in the kitchen because its author, Caren McSherry-Valagao is herself unpretentious, helpful and ever an inspiration. Recently at CityFood we themed an issue around "Learning to Cook in the '90s" and Caren was the first person we considered for our Interview of the Month feature. Not just because she runs an exemplary cooking school but because she embodies the true meaning of the word "teacher." Not a mere educator able to pass on a bit of information or techniques — a computer can do that much for you — but a person who can make you feel as passionate about a subject as she herself does. I have known Caren for many years and she has always been an energetic ambassadress for the joy of cooking and eating well. Her approach to food is neither devoutist nor fearful. She sees the partaking and sharing of food as the sensual enjoyment of life that it should be. She believes that ease need not compromise elegance. If she has a crumb of fanaticism it is in her standards regarding ingredients. In Caren's mind an impressive dish is not one that is technically difficult to create or bizarre in its originality, it is one that looks good and tastes absolutely wonderful. To that end she will encourage you to search out the very best—quality foodstuffs and enjoy them lavishly, not measure them out anxiously like drops of medicine. These philosophies are reflected in her recipes, which is why I have the greatest confidence in this, her first cookbook: it's practical, it will put you in an attractive position and it is guaranteed to achieve the desired results. And can you say that certain other Joy of . . . manuals always did that for you?*

All the recipes in this book are the favorites of the students at Caren's Cooking School. A dozen years ago I was one of those students. I would sit on one of the little metal folding chairs in Caren's kitchen and watch how she enrobed a Beef Wellington in puff pastry or overlapped circles of cucumber on a poached salmon to make it look nifty. From Caren I learned how to make worldly things such as mushroom duxelle and veal demi-glace, but more importantly it was Caren who woke me up to the fact that tomato soup wasn't invented in a can and how exciting the real thing can taste when you make it yourself from fresh garden produce. Today she still reminds me that it is worth the two-minute effort to make my own mayonnaise or the one-hour trip across town in search of skinny French green beans. Why? Because in a demanding and often ungrateful world, it can be these very simple things that provide your just rewards. I am certain that the users of this book will find it a reward in their day and I congratulate the author on an effort well performed.

Rhonda May,

Vancouver, B.C. September 1994

Glossary

Al Dente

This term means "to the tooth" and refers to the desired final cooking texture for pasta: cooked through but still chewy.

Arborio Rice

Risotto, a specific traditional Italian dish, is made with this short-grained rice which has a thick coating of soft starch. Gradual cooking and the slow addition of liquid dissolves the starch, and constant stirring distributes this starch to create a creamy fusion of rice and vegetables/seafood/meat. Do not rinse the rice before cooking.

Arugula

This edible "weed" was introduced to North Americans through Italian cuisines. Used fresh in green salads, it has a peppery taste.

Asiago Cheese

Asiago is a hard cow's milk cheese with a piquant flavor. It is commonly used as a grating cheese. Its home is the province of Vicenza outside Venice.

Bain Marie

Translated to "Mary's Bath" it has been considered to have been named for the Virgin Mary, the symbol of gentleness, since the term implies the gentleness of this method of cooking. It is a utensil used for keeping sauces or soups warm, for melting ingredients without burning them or for cooking dishes very slowly. The bain-marie refers to a pan filled with water in which the food-containing vessel is halfway submerged. During the cooking process, the water must not reach a boil.

Baked Blind

This cooking term refers to prebaking a pastry shell without the filling. The most common method is to cover the pastry lining with a non-scorching paper, such as parchment paper, weight the paper with raw, dried beans or clay pastry beans which will prevent the pastry from puffing up, and then bake.

Balsamic Vinegar

This unique flavor is a special treasure to Italians and a result of years of tradition and master artistry. The secret formula is passed down the family line. (At one time in history, the balsamic "mother" was considered of such value as to be included in a wedding dowry.) The Italian Government has recognized the Modena region which originally developed this treasure by granting it DOCG protection. The flavors are produced by aging the wine vinegar in 10 different woods starting with oak. Each wood imparts its own flavor. The length of time in each barrel distinguishes the balsamic vinegar. Younger balsamic vinegars are tarter; age mellows the acidity for a sweeter condiment.

Black Sesame Seeds

These have the same flavor as white sesame seeds. They are used primarily as a garnish. Store in an airtight jar in dry conditions to keep indefinitely.

Blue Corn Flour

Indigenous to the U.S. Southwest, its blue color is a naturally occurring corn variation. It indicates a higher lysine (a protein) content adding to its nutritional value. This higher protein content makes it softer and less starchy than other corns. Blue corn flour has more flavor than the regular yellow or white cornmeal.

Glossary

Bocconcini (Fresh Mozzarella)

In Italy, water-buffalo milk is used to make this unripened mozzarella. In North America, cow's milk is substituted. This cheese should ideally be eaten a few days after it has been made. The texture is firm but moist. It should be stored in water to prevent it from drying out.

Bouillon Powder

Look for a good quality bouillon powder such as the European products Maggi or Knorr-Swiss. Do not substitute a chicken bouillon cube which contains MSG.

Caperberries

These are the fruit of the wild caper bush, indigenous to the Mediterranean. They are, on average, three times the size of a small caper and usually packed in vinegar with their stems intact. They have the same salty, tart flavor as capers. They can be served like an olive, and are well suited as a cocktail accompaniment with roasted almonds.

Capers

These unopened buds from a caper bush (buds from nasturtiums are sometimes used as a substitute) are uniquely native to the Mediterranean. Small capers are generally considered to be superior to large ones both in their texture and flavor. Their salty, tart taste complements smoky foods like smoked salmon and are a wonderful addition to pasta dishes and fish.

Celery Root (Celeriac)

A variety of celery grown for its fleshy white root, it is cultivated in the north of France. To North Americans, celery root is available fresh or grated and preserved in vinegar.

Chèvre

In French this means both "goat" and "goat's milk cheese." In France chèvres are made in various sizes and shapes, and sometimes coated with herbs or ash.

Chinese Mushrooms

Usually, black, the most commonly referred-to Chinese mushroom is a dried shiitake. The highest grade has a thick, full cap, and a small white star design in the centre. The smoky flavor is a prominent seasoning in many Chinese soups and meat dishes. Dried Italian porcini mushrooms can be substituted.

Chocolate

A high cocoa content balanced with pure cocoa butter imparts the requisite rich chocolate flavour to desserts. Look for a deep dark color and glossy finish. Notice the mouth feel: it should have a smooth consistency leaving a lingering aftertaste that is not too bitter or sweet. A greyish tinge, most often found in the centre of a block of chocolate denotes, a chocolate "bloom" where the cocoa has separated from the cocoa butter. This does not necessarily indicate that the chocolate is bad; it usually means that the chocolate has been stored improperly. Use semisweet or bittersweet chocolate interchangeably, depending on your taste.

Coat Back of the Spoon

This cooking term appears in recipes for egg-based custards and sauces. It is a measuring technique to determine if the egg in the sauce is cooked. Lift the spoon (usually wooden) from the sauce, and draw your finger through the sauce on the back of the spoon. The clear space left by your finger should remain distinct.

Glossary

Copper

Historically, copper is considered to be the best material for cooking utensils because of its excellent heat conducting abilities. Copper pans distribute heat evenly allowing greater control in handling certain cooking methods. As copper destroys vitamin C, most pans are lined with tin or stainless steel.

Crostini

This term applies to thin slices of a baguette which have been toasted. The crostini are served with a savory topping such as diced tomatoes and basil.

Crystallized Flowers

French pâtissiers use these liberally to decorate cakes and pastries. Desserts look spectacular with crystallized flowers caught up in spun sugar for a festive croquembouche, or embroidered around the top and sides of celebration cakes.

Dredge

To coat a food in flour.

Dried Beans/Legumes

This food is an inexpensive and highly valuable source of protein. Dried beans have basically the same texture, however their tastes do vary, as well as their size, color and shape. When combining several beans into one dish, it is better to cook each bean separately and then to combine the cooked beans. Soaking beans only makes them more gaseous; cooking them in a covered heavy pot slowly and in a minimal amount of liquid will help temper their infamous effect. All dry beans should be stored in closed, airtight containers in a cool, dry place. Theoretically, they can be kept for years, but it is better if they are used within 6 to 9 months of purchase.

Dried Wild Mushrooms

The complex flavors of wild mushrooms add an earthy dimension to risottos and sauces. Wild mushrooms refer to any variety other than the white button mushrooms, which are domestically cultivated. Varieties include: morels, boletos, cèpes, porcini, chanterelles. Revive dried mushrooms for a few moments in water before using. Use this water in your sauce.

Dutch Processed Cocoa

This term originates with a Dutch chocolatier, Van Houten, who discovered that adding an alkali to cocoa would stabilize the rich dark color and flavor. Dutch cocoa is less acidic, ensuring a purer chocolate flavor.

Edible Flowers

The following flowers are recognized as being edible as they contain no toxins: Johnny-jump-ups, violets, roses, forget-me-nots, cornflowers and scented geranium leaves. Look for a greengrocer who sells organically grown produce.

Endive

Related to chicory, this herb is recognizable by its long, sleek leaves which are snugly wrapped to form an elongated, oval head. These leaves can be separated and served raw in thin slices, tossed into a green salad. Caution! The starches in the endive will go brown when it is sliced raw, in the same way as apples and peeled potatoes. Eaten raw, it tastes somewhat bitter. The head can be sliced and grilled.

Extra Virgin Olive Oil

Olive oil enhances the flavors of foods without overwhelming them. An extra virgin olive oil is a result of the first pressing of newly harvested olives. The leftover meat is further pressed to produce a pure olive oil, which is

a lower grade and should be reserved for frying use only. Chemicals are used to extract more oil from the remaining olive meat to produce the most inferior grade, pomace oil. There is a wide selection of extra virgin olive oils available in a wide range of prices and flavors. Try to taste many different brands to determine one that most suits your budget and taste. Extra virgin olive oil lasts for up to 6 months if kept in a cool, dark place.

Fermented Black Beans

Considered to be one of the oldest Chinese seasonings, these are black beans which have been preserved in a salty brine, then dried and fermented. They are a perfect accent to delicate foods such as poultry, vegetables and fish. Keep refrigerated in an airtight container for an indefinite shelf life.

Fiddleheads

The name refers to the distinctive coiled shape of the unopened fern. The season for this vegetable is short as it is harvested when the plant is still young, in the late spring. This fern favors wet, humid and cooler climates, such as the coast of BC. The flavor is astringent, yet earthy.

Fish Sauce

This condiment or seasoning comes from South East Asia and is made from fish, usually anchovies and mackerel, fermented in salt. It is a dark brown liquid, most readily available to North Americans as the Thai sauce, nam pla.

Five Blend Peppercorns

This colorful mixture of peppercorns is designed to add a complex pepper flavour to food preparations. The mixture includes white, black, green and pink peppercorns and allspice. The allspice creates a distinct sweet flavor characteristic.

French Flan Pan

Pâtissiers use this ring made of tin plate for preparing tarts and flans. When placed on a baking sheet in the oven, it assures better distribution of heat through the pastry and enables the cooked tart or flan to be easily removed.

Gelatin Sheets

This is the European version of Knox gelatin powder. The superiortity of the sheets is their ability to dissolve evenly and not in the lumpy style of the powder. This makes them much easier to use. Six gelatin sheets is equivalent to one tablespoon of gelatin powder.

Greek Olives

Although originating in the same country as kalamata olives, these olives are not almond shaped and are not slit before the brine curing and packing in vinegar. This makes the flesh more firm. Both olives are ripened to the same black-purple colour.

Herbs & Spices

It is important to know that flavors are particularly vulnerable to light and heat. Store your herbs and spices in cool, dry and dark places for longer flavor life.

Icing Sugar

Also called confectioner's sugar, this is very finely ground white sugar blended with corn starch, generally used to make frostings.

Kalamata Olives

These black pruple olives are identifiable by their distinctive slit and almond shape. They are cured in brine and packed with vinegar. The slit enables better penetration of the brine making the flesh quite soft.

Glossary

Mascarpone

This is a rich, sweet cream cheese is from the Lombardy region in Italy. It is made from cow's milk and is ivory-colored, soft, delicate, and double to triple cream richness. The flavor association can range from clotted cream to butter. This versatile cheese blends well with other flavors.

Nicoise Olives

A tasty, quite small olive indigenous to France, its colour is brown to brown-green-black. It is brine cured and often packed with herbs, stems intact.

Nuts

Categorized as dry fruits, they are identified as having a higher fat content and low water content. Nuts are valuable as a good energy source, rich in calcium and B vitamins. Their full flavors are released when they are lightly toasted immediately before eating or adding to any recipe. Preserve the highly volatile flavors by storing in an airtight container.

Pancetta

North Americans would recognize the similar cut of meat as bacon. However the Italian version, pancetta, is not smoked, only salt cured. Although recipes do invite bacon as a substitution, the flavor is remarkably different: it less greasy and has a more delicate flavor. Pancetta should be sliced very thin and can be eaten raw or cooked.

Parchment Paper

This unwaxed, thin paper is used in cooking as it stands a certain amount of heat and provides insulation. It can be used to wrap foods to be baked en papillote; to cover preparations while they are cooking so they do not brown too quickly; and to line cake tins.

Pasta

Imported pasta is superior to domestic pasta as it has a stronger texture, giving it the ability to hold its shape "al dente" longer. Each shape should be considered for its ability to carry its sauce. Fresh pasta is a tender dough, rolled into thin sheets and cut into various widths. Its tenderness lends itself well to lasagna and stuffed pasta dishes baked in the oven. Its porous surface and egg-enriched taste complement delicate flavors.

Pine Nuts

These small edible seeds of the stone pine are indigenous to the Mediterranean. Surrounded by a hard husk, the pine kernels are extracted from between the scales of the pine cones. They have a particularly high energy content and are very oily, making them go rancid very easily. They taste a little like almonds but tend to be more resinous and spicy.

Piri Piri Pepper

Original to South Africa, this pepper is "sweet hot" not "burn hot."

Radicchio

Eaten raw, this Italian red winter chicory has an astringent or tart taste and is usually served mixed with a green salad. Cooking or grilling carmelizes the astringency making it a delicious solo vegetable.

Rice Vinegar

This grain vinegar made from rice wine lees is light and sweet. It is less harsh than distilled white vinegar and less sweet than cider vinegar. It is used by the Chinese as a daily vinegar for dressings and sauces.

Glossary

Saffron

LaMancha, Spain produces the finest saffron, which is the rusty gold stigma of the purple crocus. Saffron is picked by hand and therefore commands a very high price. Fortunately, only a small amount is required to add a brilliant color and musky flavor to your dish. Before using, soak for 20 minutes in a hot liquid.

Sea Salt

This is salt in its purest form without additives. It is stronger and truer in flavor than processed salt, so less is required.

Sesame Oil

This highly aromatic oil is extracted from toasted sesame seeds. Japanese sesame oil is considered to be a superior flavor as the Chinese versions can be burnt or rancid. This oil should be stored in a cool, dark place. Use it as a seasoning oil only! Its deep flavor should be used as discreetly as a perfume. Do not use it to cook with as it has a very low burning point.

Soy Sauce

This is available in dark, sweet to light grades. The recipes in this book refer to a medium quality such as Kikkoman.

Sugar Boiler

The copper in this unlined vessel assures even heat distribution required to reach a high temperature to sufficiently melt the sugar. Unlined copper is necessary because the intense heat reached by the melted sugar can damage the metal lining which otherwise protects the copper pots.

Sun Cured Olives

Full flavored and meaty, these black and wrinkled olives are dry-salt cured and rubbed with olive oil.

Vanilla

The vanilla orchid is native to Mexico, although development has been extended into the West Indies. Mexican vanilla is the most highly prized followed by Bourbon vanilla from the West Indies, and then Tahitian. The barely ripened pods are plunged into boiling water, then sun baked to extract the vanillin crystals. Blacker pods are more fragrant as they have been sun baked longer. Chemical science has been able to fool the taste buds into sensing the vanilla flavor. This imitation vanilla flavor is a poor substitute, leaving an acrid aftertaste.

Walnut Oil

With its light, fruity taste and low cholesterol count, this oil is ideal to create sophisticated dressings for salad. Store in a dark, cool place: do not refrigerate.

Warm Water Solution

In bread making, yeast is dissolved in a warm water solution containing sugar. As yeast is a living substance, a suitable environment must exist to encourage its growth. Boiling-hot water will kill the yeast, and very cool water will retard its growth. An easy gauge to determine the ideal temperature for the water is to test it against the inside of your wrist. It should feel comfortably on the hot side against this sensitive part of your skin.

Wasabi

This powdered green horseradish, a common condiment in Japan, is served by mixing with cold water to form a paste.

Wild Rice

This reed is indigenous to the flooded plains of Manitoba. Its seed is called a rice for its comparative size, shape, the similar growing conditions to its rice cousins, and because it is cooked in the same way. This "rice" has a very rich, earthy flavor. Serve in small portions or extend by combining with other grains.

Starters

Jose's Herbed Olives

Warm Chevre Spread with Toasted Baguette

Layered Mascarpone Torta

Herbed Cheese Appetizers

Grilled Zucchini Rolls

Proscuitto-Parmesan Fingers

Quesadillas with Black Bean Salsa

Blue Corn Fritters

Corn Cakes & Grilled Scallops with Red Pepper Sauce

West Coast Crab Cakes

Santa Fe Chicken

Marinated Lamb on Rosemary Skewers

Chicken Satay

Bloody Gazpacho

Fiddlehead & Spinach Soup

Celery & Stilton Soup

Provencal Seafood Soup

Shrimp Wonton Soup

Tuscan Bean Soup with Tomato Crostini

Vegetable & Lentil Soup

Tortellini & Chorizo Soup

Fresh Pumpkin Soup with Toasted Hazelnuts

Field Greens with Asian Dressing

Creamy Garlic Dressing

New Wave Nicoise

Caesar Salad with Herbed Garlic Croutons

Spinach Salad in Bread Bowls

Crisp Iceberg with Roasted Garlic Dressing

Cress, Apple & Endive Salad

Northern Italian Bean Salad

Rice & Black Bean Salad with Ancho Chili Dressing

Asian Vegetable & Noodle Salad with Ginger Dressing

Cold Duck Pasta Salad

Roasted Chicken Salad with Tropical Salsa

Jose's Herbed Olives

My husband José loves to make these olives in large batches.

Fresh woody-stemmed herbs—rosemary, oregano and thyme—are "bruised" or lightly crushed rather than chopped.

Ingredients

- 2 or 3 cloves garlic, chopped
- $\frac{1}{2}$ lemon, cut into slices
- 1 tablespoon hot chili flakes
- 1 tablespoon coarsely cracked pepper
- 2 or 3 sprigs fresh rosemary, bruised
- 2 or 3 sprigs fresh oregano, bruised
- 2 or 3 sprigs fresh thyme, bruised
- 1 cup niçoise olives
- 1 cup kalamata olives
- 1 cup sun-dried, oil-cured olives
- 1 cup large green olives, with pits
- 1 cup olive oil

Method

1. In a large bowl, mix together the garlic, lemon slices, chili flakes, cracked pepper, rosemary, oregano and thyme.

2. Add the olives, stirring well to combine the flavors.

3. Pack the olives into canning jars and refrigerate until ready to use for up to 7 days. The olives can also be served right away.

Makes 4 cups

 Dry Fino Sherry

Warm Chevre Spread with Toasted Baguette

This chunky spread, featuring sun-dried tomatoes, artichokes, olives and creamy chèvre, is a fabulous blend of flavors.

It also makes a wonderful sauce when tossed with your favorite cooked pasta.

Ingredients

1	head garlic
3/4	cup sun-dried tomatoes
1/3	cup olive oil
1	medium onion, sliced
1	tablespoon granulated sugar
1/2 to 1	cup dry white wine
8	ounces chèvre
4	ounces firm cream cheese
1	jar (14 oz.) artichoke hearts, drained and cut into eighths
2/3	cup niçoise olives
1	tablespoon coarsely cracked pepper

Slices of toasted baguette or crusty
French bread

Method

1. Preheat oven to 325°. Cut 1/4 inch off the top of the garlic head and rub the entire head with olive oil. Place in a garlic roaster or wrap loosely in foil. Bake for 45 minutes to 1 hour, depending on the size of the garlic, or until the cloves are soft and golden brown. When cool enough to handle, squeeze the garlic pulp out into a bowl and set aside.

2. Meanwhile, cut the tomatoes into a medium dice and soak in enough hot water to cover for about 15 minutes until softened. Drain and set aside.

3. Heat the oil in a sauté pan. When the oil is hot, add the onions and cook for about 3 minutes until they begin to brown. Add the sugar and continue to cook for about 10 minutes or until the onions are dark brown and nicely caramelized. Pour in the wine and deglaze the pan, scraping all the brown flavor bits from the bottom.

4. Add the chèvre, cream cheese, tomatoes, artichokes, reserved garlic, olives and pepper. Stir until the cheeses melt and the entire mixture is creamy and smooth. If it is too thick, simply adjust the consistency with the addition of more wine. Taste and adjust seasonings.

5. Transfer to a serving bowl and offer alongside slices of toasted baguette or crusty French bread.

Serves 8 to 10

 White Port, chilled

Layered Mascarpone Torta

The flavors from three types of cheese combine beautifully to create this layered appetizer.

Or, try serving the torta as the perfect finale to dinner with a glass of port.

Ingredients

16 ounces cream cheese

8 ounces Bavarian blue cheese, Gorgonzola or cambazola

8 ounces mascarpone cheese

1 cup pignolas or European pine nuts, toasted

3/4 cup sun-dried tomatoes

1 bunch fresh basil, washed and dried

Method

1. Have all the cheeses at room temperature. Line a 7-inch springform pan with plastic wrap, letting enough hang over so that you can cover the top of the torta when finished. Spread half of the cream cheese evenly over the bottom of the lined pan. Reserve the remaining half.

2. Remove and discard any rind from the blue cheese. Place the cheese in a bowl and mix it until smooth. Spread this over the cream cheese layer.

3. Finely chop the sun-dried tomatoes and mix together with the mascarpone cheese. Spread evenly over the top of the blue cheese. Arrange the basil leaves in a single layer on top; you will need about 12 large leaves. Save the smaller leaves for garnishing.

4. Divide the remaining cream cheese into thirds. Spread two-thirds of the cream cheese over the top of the last layer. Reserve the last one-third for garnish.

5. Fold the excess plastic wrap over top of the torta and chill for about 4 hours or until firmly set.

6. To serve, release the torta from the pan. Open the plastic wrap and place a serving plate on top of the torta. Invert it and peel off the remaining plastic wrap. Remove the bottom of the springform pan.

7. Press in all but a few of the toasted pine nuts all the way around the side of the torta. Spoon the reserved one-third remaining cream cheese into a piping bag fitted with a small star tip. Pipe a series of rosettes on the top of the torta and garnish each rosette with a small basil leaf and a pine nut.

Serves 12 to 15

 1977 Kopke Colheita Porto

Herbed Cheese Appetizers

My good friend Cindy Burridge gave me this recipe. Her version, which calls for bocanncini (fresh mozzarella), is fabulous but I have changed the cheese to cream cheese so that these appetizers can be made ahead and hold for several hours.

Ingredients

²/₃ cup extra virgin olive oil

1 tablespoon *each* dried basil, oregano, thyme and rosemary

1 to 2 teaspoons ground five-blend peppercorns

1 8-ounce package firm cream cheese

18 medium sun-dried tomatoes

36 small or medium fresh basil leaves

Small toothpicks

Method

1. Pour the oil into a shallow 8-inch square pan. Add the rosemary, oregano, thyme and pepper, stirring to combine.

2. Cut the cream cheese into small 1/2-inch cubes (you should have 36). Add to the oil mixture, tossing lightly so that each cube is liberally coated with the mixture. Set aside at room temperature for about 2 hours.

3. Meanwhile, place the tomatoes in a bowl with enough boiling water to cover. Set aside for about 15 minutes to soften. Drain, blot dry and cut in half.

4. Take a toothpick and thread on one of the basil leaves. Thread on a piece of cheese and a piece of tomato, too. Repeat with remaining ingredients.

5. Arrange the appetizers on a colorful platter and serve at room temperature.

Serves 8 to 12

Merryvale Napa Valley Meritage

Grilled Zucchini Rolls

Ricotta cheese, sun-dried tomatoes, capers and fresh herbs combine to make the filling for this great appetizer, making a fresh addition to any antipasto platter.

Ingredients

Filling

1/4   cup sun-dried tomatoes

1   cup ricotta cheese

3   tablespoons capers, chopped

1   tablespoon chopped fresh oregano

3   tablespoons snipped fresh chives

1   teaspoon sea salt

1   teaspoon freshly ground pepper

2   large, firm zucchinis

   Olive oil

   Shavings of Parmesan cheese

Method

1. Place the tomatoes in a bowl and add enough boiling water to cover. Set aside for about 10 minutes until softened.

2. Drain, blot dry and coarsely chop tomatoes. Set aside.

3. Meanwhile, combine the ricotta, capers, oregano, chives, salt and pepper, stirring to combine. Add the reserved tomatoes and mix well. Set aside.

4. Trim the ends off the zucchinis. Using a slicing knife, carefully slice the zucchinis lengthwise into 1/8-inch-thick slices. If you have a mandoline, it works great.

5. Lightly brush the zucchini slices with olive oil and grill for about 1 minute per side, turning once, or until golden and soft enough to roll. (You can also do this in a wide frying pan.) Set aside.

6. Lay the zucchini slices on a work surface. Spoon about 1 tablespoon of filling onto one end of each slice. Roll up the zucchini, beginning with the end covered with cheese, and secure with a toothpick, if necessary.

7. Arrange on a decorative platter and garnished with shavings of Parmesan cheese to serve.

Serves 4 to 8

Prosciutto-Parmesan Fingers

Crisp phyllo is wrapped around thin slices of prosciutto that have been seasoned with sweet mustard and Parmesan cheese. These appetizers can easily be frozen and baked directly out of the freezer.

Ingredients

3   heaping tablespoons Dijon honey mustard or other sweet mustard

$^1/_2$ cup extra virgin olive oil

12   sheets of phyllo

24   thin slices of prosciutto

1   cup freshly grated Parmesan cheese

Freshly ground five-blend peppercorns

1   wooden dowel, 14 to 18 inches long and about the diameter of your index finger

Method

1. Combine the mustard and the olive oil and set aside.

2. Using one sheet of phyllo at a time (and keeping the other sheets covered until use), open up a sheet of phyllo onto the work surface. Brush it evenly with the mustard mixture.

3. Tear a slice of prosciutto into pieces and scatter them over the mustard. It is not important that the mustard be covered completely.

4. Sprinkle some Parmesan cheese over the prosciutto and some freshly ground pepper.

5. Beginning with the edge nearest you, fold the sheet up and over by 2 inches. Lay the dowel along the folded end nearest you.

6. Roll the sheet of phyllo around the dowel, jelly-roll-fashion, until you reach the far side. Push the phyllo "finger" off the dowel and lightly squeeze it so that it sticks together. Slide the phyllo onto a lightly greased baking sheet.

7. Repeat with remaining phyllo and other ingredients.

8. Preheat oven to 400°. Cut the phyllo "fingers" in half, crosswise on the diagonal, and bake them for 10 to 15 minutes or until they turn golden brown and crisp. Serve hot or at room temperature.

Serves 8

 Chianti Classico such as Salcetino

Quesadillas with Black Bean Salsa

Transform ordinary quesadillas into something festive by offering this colorful salsa, made with black turtle beans, jalapeño pepper and avocado, as an accompaniment.

Ingredients

Beans

1	cup black turtle beans
1	yellow pepper, seeded and diced
$1/2$	bunch chopped fresh cilantro
$1/2$	cup diced sweet onion
	Juice of 1 fresh lemon
1	teaspoon sea salt
2	cloves minced garlic
3	tablespoons olive oil
$1/2$	jalapeño pepper, finely diced
1	avocado

Quesadillas

1	package (10) 8-inch flour tortillas
$1/2$	pound jack cheese, sliced
$1/2$	pound Brie or Camembert, rind removed, sliced
1	10-ounce can poblano chilies, drained and chopped
	Oil for brushing tortillas

Method

BEANS

1. To quick-cook the beans, place them in a large pot and cover them with cold water. Cover and bring to a boil. Drain the beans, put them back in the pot, and cover with fresh cold water. Again, cover the pot and bring beans to a boil.

2. As soon as they reach the boil, drain them again and cover with fresh water. Cover and bring to a boil for the third time.

3. Reduce heat and simmer for about 40 minutes or until the beans are cooked to your liking. Drain and set aside to cool.

4. Combine the beans, yellow pepper, cilantro, onion, lemon juice, garlic, oil, jalapeño pepper and salt.

5. Peel and dice the avocado and add to the salsa, stirring to combine. Taste and adjust seasonings; chill until ready to serve.

QUESADILLAS

6. Heat a nonstick fry pan, place a tortilla in the pan warm it on both sides for about 1 minute. Place a few slices of each cheese on one side of the tortilla. Sprinkle about one tablespoon of chilies over the cheese. Fold the tortilla over and brush lightly with oil.

7. Brown on both sides, about 1 minute each, or until the cheese is soft and melted. Cut in wedges and serve with the black bean salsa

Serves 6 to 8 generously

 Microbrewery beer, such as Granville Island

Blue Corn Fritters

Traditional corn fritters are an old-fashioned favorite, but in this version I use stone-ground blue cornmeal. A dusting of icing sugar adds a different yet delicious twist.

Ingredients

1	pound frozen corn kernels (or freshly cooked corn)
2	eggs
2	green onions, finely chopped
1	small clove garlic, minced
3	tablespoons chopped cilantro
1/2	yellow onion, finely chopped
1/2	cup plus 2 tablespoons unbleached flour
1/3	cup blue cornmeal
1 1/2	teaspoons fine sea salt
1 1/2	teaspoons granulated sugar
2	teaspoons baking powder
2	teaspoons ground coriander
1/4	teaspoon freshly ground pepper

Oil, for frying

Icing sugar

Method

1. Place the corn in a colander and thaw completely. Set aside to drain.

2. Transfer corn to a food processor fitted with a metal blade and pulse 10 or 15 times, taking care not to purée but to leave some texture to the corn. Transfer to a mixing bowl and set aside.

3. Lightly beat the eggs and add to the corn. Add the green onion, garlic, cilantro and yellow onion, stirring to combine.

4. Meanwhile, heat the oil to a temperature of 400°.

5. Combine the flour, blue cornmeal, salt, granulated sugar, baking powder, coriander and pepper, stirring to mix.

6. Add dry ingredients to the corn mixture, stirring until well blended.

7. When oil is hot, drop the corn mixture by tablespoons into the oil, a few at a time, and fry for 4 to 5 minutes or until golden brown on all sides.

8. Drain on paper towels and dust with icing sugar before serving.

Serves 8 to 10

Microbrewery beer, such as Whistler Brewery

Corn Cakes & Grilled Scallops with Red Pepper Sauce

These little corn cakes are made special with the addition of marinated, grilled sea scallops. You could, however top

them with a prawn, crab claw or simply enjoy them on their own embellished with the very fragrant and slightly spicy red pepper sauce.

Ingredients

Sauce

2   tablespoons olive oil

3   shallots, chopped

1   14-ounce jar (14 oz.) roasted red peppers, drained

$^1/_2$ teaspoon ground cumin

1   tablespoon hot chili powder

$^1/_4$ teaspoon Mexican oregano

1 $^1/_2$ tablespoons balsamic vinegar

$^1/_4$ teaspoon sea salt

Corn Cakes

3   large russet potatoes, peeled

1   12-ounce can kernel corn, drained

2   shallots, chopped

$^1/_4$ cup snipped chives

2   tablespoon mayonnaise

1   heaping tablespoons Dijon mustard

1   egg lightly beaten

1 to 2 teaspoons piri piri sauce or Tabasco

$^1/_2$ teaspoon sea salt

1   teaspoon freshly ground pepper

1   pound fresh sea scallops

$^1/_3$ cup olive oil

2   cloves garlic, minced

1   teaspoon sea salt

Method

SAUCE

1. For the sauce, heat the oil in a small fry pan. When oil is hot, add the shallots and sauté for 3 minutes until soft. Transfer to a food processor fitted with a metal blade and add the peppers, cumin, chili, oregano, balsamic and salt. Process into a purée, taste and adjust seasonings. Set aside.

CORN CAKES

2. Cook the potatoes in boiling water until soft. Drain and return them to the pot over low heat to let them dry out for just a minute or so. Remove and let cool. Then grate potatoes into a large bowl and set aside.

3. Heat a cast iron pan over high heat. Add the drained corn and roast, shaking the pan occasionally, until corn is browned and slightly dried out. Set aside.

4. Combine the corn with the potatoes. Add the shallots, chives, mayonnaise, mustard, egg, piri piri, salt and pepper. Shape the mixture into 24 small cakes.

5. Heat a nonstick skillet. When hot, add the cakes, a few at a time, and cook for 5 to 7 minutes, turning once, or until golden on both sides. Transfer to a serving platter and keep warm.

6. Combine the 1/3 cup olive oil, garlic and salt. Add the scallops, tossing to coat. Heat a grill or frying pan to high. Grill the scallops on both sides, for about 4 minutes or until they turn translucent.

7. Arrange the grilled scallops on top of the corn cake and serve with some of the red pepper sauce alongside.

Serves 6 to 8

 Henri Bourgeois Sancerre

West Coast Crab Cakes

Crab cakes are fast becoming popular not only here in Vancouver, but all over North America. What separates good from bad? CRAB!

Please, never substitute imitation crab meat, always use Dungeness and plenty of it. If not, you simply have a potato cake.

Ingredients

1   large russet potato, cooked, peeled and grated

1   large egg, beaten

2   tablespoons mayonnaise

1   heaping tablespoon Dijon mustard

1   teaspoon piri piri sauce

1   green onion, finely chopped

2   tablespoons chopped fresh chives

¼   cup fresh red pepper, diced

¾   pound fresh Dungeness crab meat
    Sea salt
    Freshly ground pepper to taste

1   cup toasted ground hazelnuts
    Unsalted butter and peanut oil in equal portions for frying

Method

1. In a large bowl, combine the grated potato, beaten egg, mayo, mustard, onion, chives, red pepper, piri piri, salt and pepper. Mix to incorporate the ingredients.

2. Mix in the crab meat, adjust the seasonings. Form the mixture into patties and roll the edges in the toasted ground hazelnuts. Press the nuts into the edges so they adhere.

3. Heat a frying pan to medium, add equal portions of butter and oil—about 1 tablespoon of each to start. Fry the cakes on both sides until golden brown, about 1 to 2 minutes each side. Serve warm.

Makes 24

 Crisp Sauvignon Blanc

Santa Fe Chicken

This colorful, flavorful dish can be served as an appetizer or as a main course served with steaming rice.

I particularly like it with blue corn chips; just digging in. I warn you, it's very hard to stop.

Ingredients

1/2	cup olive oil
1	yellow onion diced (about 1 cup)
4	garlic cloves, minced
2	red bell peppers, seeded and diced
1	14-ounce can kernel corn, drained
3	boneless chicken breasts, skinned and cut into bite-size pieces

2 to 3 tablespoons hot chili powder

1	teaspoon ground cumin
1/2	bunch cilantro, chopped
1	teaspoon hot pepper flakes

Warm flour tortillas or corn chips

Method

1. Heat 1/4 cup of the oil in a wide sauté pan. When the oil is hot, add the onion and 2 of the garlic cloves. Cook for about 5 minutes or until softened. Add the red peppers and corn and cook over medium heat for 5 more minutes or until vegetables are soft. Remove and set aside.

2. In the same pan, heat the remaining 1/4 cup of oil. When the oil is hot, add the 2 remaining garlic cloves along with the chicken. Cook, turning occasionally, for about 10 minutes or until well browned. Stir in the chili, cumin, cilantro and optional chili flakes.

3. Add the reserved pepper-corn mixture and heat through to blend the flavors. Taste and season with salt.

4. Serve on a decorative platter garnished with wedges of warm flour tortillas or corn chips.

Serves 6

 your choice of Mexican beer, such as Pacifico

Marinated Lamb on Rosemary Skewers

These tiny appetizer kebabs are unique, due to the fact that rosemary branches are used in place of wooden skewers. This not only gives a subtle internal essence of rosemary to the lamb, but provides a very interesting conversation piece.

Ingredients

- 18 sprigs of rosemary (2 to 3 inches long), preferably older stalks
- 1 lamb loin (about 1 pound), trimmed of any fat
- 2 heaping tablespoons Dijon mustard
- 2 cloves garlic, minced
- 1/4 cup olive oil
- 2 teaspoons coarsely ground pepper
- Sea salt

Method

1. Take the rosemary sprigs and strip them of the needles, leaving about 1/4 inch of needles on one end of each stalk. Set stalks aside. Finely chop the leaves (you will need about 2 teaspoons) and set aside.

2. Cut the lamb into 1-inch cubes and place in a shallow dish.

3. Combine the mustard, garlic, oil, pepper, reserved chopped rosemary and salt, to taste. Mix well to combine. Spoon over the lamb and mix well until coated. Cover and marinate in the refrigerator for 2 to 6 hours.

4. Heat a grill or barbecue to medium heat. Lift meat from marinade (reserve marinade) and carefully skewer onto the stripped rosemary sprigs, leaving the leaf end on top.

5. Grill the skewered lamb, taking care not to overcook it, for about 2 minutes per side, turning once. Serve hot or at room temperature.

Serves 6 to 8

 Cabernet Sauvignon such as Duckhorn

Chicken Satay

The popular Indonesian appetizer can be made with beef or pork or chicken, as it is here. The peanut butter sauce is the distinguishing ingredient in this sauce.

Ingredients

2   whole boneless chicken breasts, skin removed

16 or so, 5-inch skewers, pre-soaked

Marinade

2   tablespoons brown sugar

$^1/_4$ cup dark molasses

$^1/_2$ cup soy sauce

Juice of 1/2 lemon

2   cloves garlic, minced

Sauce

1   small onion, diced

1 or 2 red chilies, chopped

2   cloves garlic, minced

1   lemon

2   teaspoons brown sugar

3   tablespoons peanut oil

4   tablespoons smooth-style peanut butter

1   tablespoon shredded kaffir lime leaf (or teaspoon grated lemon rind)

2   teaspoons lemon juice

1   cup coconut milk

$^1/_4$ cup chopped cilantro, for garnish

Method

1. Cut the chicken into 1/2-inch cubes. Thread 4 or 5 pieces of chicken onto each skewer. Lay them in a wide shallow dish.

2. For the marinade, combine the sugar, molasses, soy, lemon juice and garlic, stirring to mix ingredients. Pour this mixture over the skewered chicken, cover and set aside to marinate for at least 30 minutes.

3. Meanwhile, for the sauce, place the onion, chilies, garlic, lemon and sugar in a food processor fitted with a metal blade. Process until puréed.

4. Heat the oil in a small saucepan. When the oil is hot, add the purée and cook for 2 to 3 minutes or just until it becomes fragrant. Add the peanut butter, lime leaf, lemon juice and coconut milk, stirring to combine. Bring to a boil, the reduce the heat and simmer for about 10 minutes or until the sauce is thick and smooth.

5. Meanwhile, grill the skewered chicken over medium heat (or coals) for 10 to 5 minutes, turning as needed.

6. To serve, arrange skewers on a decorative platter and spoon some of the sauce over the chicken. Garnish with chopped cilantro and serve immediately.

Serves 4 to 8

 Pinot Blanc

Bloody Gazpacho

Cold soup on a hot summer afternoon is always a treat. With our society turning towards a diet that includes a bigger variety of vegetables, this old favorite puts on a new face with the accompaniment of a frozen bottle of vodka. Bring on the vegetarian summer!

Ingredients

2	English cucumbers
1	green pepper, diced
1	red pepper , diced
4	large ripe tomatoes, diced
1	stalk celery, diced
8	green onions, sliced very thin
2	cloves garlic, minced
2	cups tomato juice
1	cup Clamato juice
2	tablespoons extra virgin olive oil
$^1/_4$	cup balsamic vinegar
1	tablespoon creamy horseradish
1 to 2	teaspoons worcestershire sauce
	Sea salt
	Freshly ground pepper
	Piri piri sauce, optional
$^1/_2$	cup chopped fresh basil
	Frozen vodka

Method

1. Peel and cut the cucumber into 1/4-inch dice. In a large stainless or glass bowl place the cucumber, both peppers, tomatoes, celery, green onions, garlic, tomato juice, Clamato juice, olive oil, balsamic, horseradish, Worcestershire. Stir well to combine all the ingredients.

2. Season with the salt and pepper and optional piri piri if you like it spicy.

3. Chill the soup for at least 4 hours or overnight. If you find it too thick, adjust with the addition of water, vegetable stock or more juice.

4. To prepare the frozen vodka, take a 2-quart milk carton, cut the top off. Set the bottle of vodka inside the milk carton and fill it to the top with water, leaving the bottleneck exposed for pouring. If you have any flower petals stick them in the water. Freeze until firm. Peel off the milk carton and serve the frozen vodka with the soup.

Serves 6 to 8

 Fume Blanc

Fiddlehead & Spinach Soup

The fresh, earthy aroma of fiddleheads combines with spinach, rice and a mélange of vegetables

in this wonderful soup. Try serving with slices of Olive-Basil Bread. When not in season, fiddleheads are available frozen.

Ingredients

3 to 4	tablespoons olive oil
1	medium yellow onion, diced
1	large carrot, peeled and diced
1	small turnip, peeled and diced
3	shallots, finely chopped
1	stalk celery, diced
3	cups fiddleheads
1/2	cup long grain rice
8	cups rich chicken stock
1	bunch spinach, washed and stemmed
2	teaspoons dried tarragon
1	teaspoon dried basil
	Sea salt
	Freshly ground pepper
	Fresh chives
	Diced beet or fresh flowers

Method

1. Heat the oil in a large soup pot over medium heat. When oil is hot, add the onion, carrot, turnip, shallots and celery. Cover the pot and let vegetables sweat for 5 to 8 minutes or until they are soft but not brown.

2. Add the fiddleheads, rice, stock, spinach, tarragon and basil. Cover, reduce heat and simmer for about 15 minutes or until the rice is cooked through.

3. Transfer mixture to a food processor fitted with a metal blade. Process until the soup is puréed. Taste and adjust seasonings with salt and pepper.

4. Ladle the soup into bowls, garnish with chives and/or the beets and edible flowers.

Serves 6 to 8

 Blanc de Blancs

Celery & Stilton Soup

The fruitiness of aged port complements the intense flavor of Stilton cheese in this rich soup, making it the perfect starter to a winter dinner by the fire. To intensify the flavor, make the soup a day in advance.

Ingredients

4   tablespoons unsalted butter (divided)

7 or 8 stalks celery, sliced (about 4 cups)

1   large onion, chopped

3   cups rich chicken stock

3   tablespoons all-purpose flour

1   bay leaf

8   ounces Stilton, Gorgonzola or
     Roquefort cheese

1   small carrot, peeled and julienned

1   cup whole milk

1   cup light cream

1   teaspoon freshly ground pepper

     Pinch of sea salt

1/2 cup port

Method

1. Melt 3 tablespoons of the butter in a heavy-bottomed pot. Add the celery and onion, cover and cook over medium heat for about 5 minutes or until the vegetables have sweated.

2. Add 2 cups of the chicken stock, cover and simmer for 20 to 25 minutes longer or until the vegetables are tender. Purée the vegetables in batches in a food processor fitted with a metal blade, until smooth. Set aside.

3. In the same soup pot, melt the remaining tablespoon of butter. Add the flour, stirring together, and cook for 3 to 4 minutes to make a roux. Whisk in the remaining cup of chicken stock along with the puréed vegetable mixture until the soup is smooth. Add the bay leaf and let the soup simmer over low heat for about 25 minutes.

4. Meanwhile, using a fork, mash the cheese into a smooth paste and set aside. Blanch the carrot in boiling water for about 1 minute, then refresh in cold water, drain and set aside for the garnish.

5. When the soup is cooked, stir in the cheese, milk and cream, taking care not to let the soup boil or it will curdle. Remove the bay leaf, taste and season with salt and pepper.

6. To serve, ladle the soup into small bowls, garnish with the julienne of carrot and a splash of port.

Serves 8

 Beaujolais

Provencal Seafood Soup

This main course soup has all the flavor of the Mediterranean. The stock creates the main essence.

Use your favorite fish but ensure you include at least 2 varieties of shellfish for that Provençal touch.

Ingredients

¹/₂	cup olive oil
2	large Spanish onions, sliced
4	garlic cloves, minced
1	medium fennel bulb, sliced, (save the fronds)
1	large leek, sliced, white part only
1	bunch fresh parsley, chopped
1	large bay leaf
1	tablespoon dried thyme
	One 2-by-1-inch strip orange peel
2	teaspoons saffron threads, pounded
2	cups white wine
2	cups Clamato juice
2	cups fish stock
2	cups canned plum tomatoes, chopped
1	red pepper, julienned
1	pound whole prawns, preferably head on
2	pounds, halibut, snapper or cod, cut into pieces
1	pound scrubbed mussels
	Sea salt
	Freshly cracked pepper
¹/₂	bunch fresh cilantro, chopped
	Piri-piri sauce to taste (optional)

Method

1. In a large pot heat the olive oil, add the onions, garlic, fennel & leek. Sauté until they become limp, add the parsley, bay leaf, thyme, orange peel and saffron. Pour in the wine & simmer for about 5 min. Add the Clamato, fish stock, chopped tomatoes & red pepper. Continue to cook for an additional 10 minutes.

2. Add the prawns and simmer covered for 3 minutes. Add the pieces of fish along with the mussels and cook covered for about 3 to 4 minutes, depending on the thickness of the fish.

3. Adjust the seasoning to suit your taste. Serve with the piri-piri sauce and a generous sprinkle of fresh cilantro or chopped fennel fronds. Garlic toasts make a nice accompaniment.

Serves 8

 Jean Durup Petit Chablis

Shrimp Wonton Soup

Finely minced shrimp meat is seasoned and compacted into little wontons to take the focus in this surprisingly easy-to-prepare soup. A bit of time is required to actually stuff the wontons, so make extra and freeze some for next time.

Ingredients

Filling

1	pound shrimp, peeled
2	fresh water chestnuts, peeled
1/2	teaspoon sea salt
	Pinch of sugar
1	tablespoon sesame oil
1	tablespoon soy sauce
1	teaspoon piri piri sauce or Tabasco
1	egg white
1	clove garlic, minced
2	tablespoons minced fresh ginger
1	green onion, finely chopped
1	8-ounce package wonton wrappers

Stock

8	cups chicken stock
2	tablespoons minced fresh ginger
1	tablespoon soy sauce
1	tablespoon fish sauce
1	tablespoon rice vinegar
15	snow peas, strings removed and cut in half
1/2	bunch cilantro, chopped
1	tablespoon pure sesame oil

Method

1. To make wontons, place the shrimp, water chestnuts, salt, sugar, sesame oil, soy, piri piri, egg white, garlic, ginger and green onion in a food processor fitted with a metal blade. Pulse well to combine all the ingredients.

2. Hold a wonton wrapper in the palm of your hand. Spoon about 1/2 tablespoon of filling into the center and squeeze the wrapper around the filling, making little purses or pouches. Set aside onto a floured surface. (Filled wontons can be frozen at this point until ready to use.)

3. Meanwhile, place the stock, ginger, soy, fish sauce and vinegar in a large soup pot. Bring to a boil, add the wontons and cook for about 2 to 3 minutes or until they float to the surface.

4. Remove the wontons with a slotted spoon and place in individual serving bowls. Drop the snow peas in to the boiling stock and let them boil no more than 1 minute. Remove from heat. Stir in sesame oil.

5. Ladle the stock and a few snow peas into each bowl and garnish with the chopped cilantro.

Serves 6

 Pinot Blanc

New Wave Nicoise Salad (page 42)

Beets and Chevre on Mixed Greens (page 45)

Tuscan Bean Soup with Crostini (page 37)

West Coast Crab Cakes (page 24)

Pictured on page 35

Tuscan Bean Soup with Crostini

Hearty, good tasting and a meal in itself, a bowl of Tuscan Bean Soup is the perfect choice for warming guests'

appetites on a cold evening. I top this version with a tomato-covered crostini just before serving.

Ingredients

1	pound white navy beans
1/3	cup olive oil
1	medium yellow onion, diced
1	large carrot, peeled and diced
2	stalks celery, diced
2	medium-size leeks (white part only), diced
3	cloves garlic, minced
6	large roma tomatoes
2	sprigs thyme
8	cups rich chicken stock
1	teaspoon sea salt
2	teaspoons freshly ground pepper

Crostini

1/2	thin loaf French bread, thinly sliced and toasted
1/2	cup sun-dried tomatoes, finely chopped
1/2	bunch parsley, minced

Method

1. Place the beans in a large pot, cover with plenty of cold water and bring to a boil. Drain the beans as soon as they come to a boil. Cover them again with fresh cold water and bring to a boil again.

2. As soon as they reach the boiling point, drain them again. Repeat with the fresh cold water, brining them to a boil for the third time.

3. Cover and cook on low heat for about 30 minutes or until the beans are cooked through. Drain.

4. Transfer 2 cups of the cooked beans to a food processor fitted with metal blade. Process into a purée. Set the whole beans and the bean purée aside.

5. Meanwhile, heat the olive oil in a soup pot. Add the onion, carrot, celery and leek. Cover and sweat the vegetables for about 10 minutes or until they become soft. Add the garlic, reserved whole beans, reserved bean purée, tomatoes, stock, thyme, salt and pepper.

6. Cover and simmer for 20 to 30 minutes. Taste and adjust seasonings.

7. Meanwhile, spoon 1 tablespoon chopped tomatoes onto each slice of toasted bread. Ladle the soup into wide individual soup bowls. Float the crostini on top and garnish with a sprinkling of parsley.

Serves 8 to 10

 Bardolino

Vegetable & Lentil Soup

Oh, the simmering aroma of a wintery pot of soup. What could be more inviting and better comfort food than homemade soup and fresh bread from the oven. Don't forget the wine by the crackling fire.

Ingredients

1/3	cup olive oil
1	large yellow onion, diced
2	leeks (white part only), finely chopped
3	cloves garlic, minced
2	carrots, peeled and diced
2	celery stalks, diced
1	small turnip, peeled and diced
10	cups rich chicken stock
1	large bay leaf
2	teaspoons dried basil
2	teaspoons dried oregano
2	teaspoons dried thyme
1	tablespoon coarsely ground pepper
2	cups lentils
1	cup green beans, sliced
1	medium zucchini, cut into large dice
1	small head cauliflower, broken into flowerettes
1	cup mushrooms, quartered
	Sea salt
	Grated Parmesan cheese

Method

1. Heat the oil in a large soup pot. Add the onion, leek and garlic. Cook over medium heat, covered but stirring occasionally, for about 8 minutes or until vegetables have sweated and are soft.

2. Add the carrots, celery and turnip to the pot, stirring to combine. Cover and continue to cook for an additional 5 minutes.

3. Pour in the stock and add the bay leaf, basil, oregano, thyme, pepper and lentils. Cover and simmer for 20 to 30 minutes.

4. Add the the beans, zucchini, cauliflower and mushrooms. Taste and adjust seasonings with salt.

5. Simmer for about 5 minutes or until the fresh vegetables are cooked through.

6. Ladle into individual bowls and garnish with freshly grated Parmesan cheese.

Serves 8 to 10

 Valpolicella

ortellini & Chorizo Soup

This soup is not only fast, easy and fresh. It's very tasty.

Eliminate the Chorizo and use vegetable stock and you can please all your meatless friends.

Ingredients

2	tablespoons olive oil
1	large yellow onion diced
1	clove garlic, minced
1	pound chorizo or other firm sausage, sliced $^1/_2$-inch thick
6	cups rich chicken stock
1	12 ounce package cheese tortellini
1	bunch spinach, washed, stems removed and chopped
	Sea salt
	Coursely ground pepper
	Freshly grated Parmesan cheese

Method

1. Heat the olive oil in a heavy skillet. When hot, add the onion and sauté for 4 to 5 minutes until golden. Add the garlic and chorizo and continue to sauté for about 5 minutes until browned.

2. Heat the stock in a soup pot. Add the tortellini and cook for about 10 minutes. Stir in the spinach and chorizo-onion mixture. Reduce heat and simmer for about 15 minutes or until the tortellini are cooked through.

3. Taste and adjust the seasonings with the salt and pepper. Ladle into bowls and pass the grated Parmesan at the table.

Serves 6

 Kunde Estate Cabernet Sauvignon

Fresh Pumpkin Soup with Toasted Hazelnuts

This lighter version of traditional pumpkin soup, made without cream, gets rave reviews,

especially when brought to the table and served from a whole pumpkin shell.

Ingredients

2	large onions, diced
1/3	cup extra virgin olive oil
1	teaspoon dried thyme
1	teaspoon dried basil
2 to 3	teaspoons freshly ground pepper
3	large carrots, peeled and cut into chunks
1/2	bunch parsley, chopped
3	large potatoes, peeled and cut into chunks
6	cups fresh pumpkin, peeled and cut into pieces
8	cups chicken stock
1/3	cup brandy
1	large pumpkin
3	tablespoons toasted ground hazelnuts

Method

1. Heat the oil in a large heavy-bottomed pot. When the oil is hot, add the onions, cover, and let them sweat for about 5 to 8 minutes until they are soft but not brown. Add the thyme, basil, pepper, carrots, parsley, potatoes, cut pumpkin and stock.

2. Bring the soup to a boil, cover and simmer for about 45 minutes, or until the vegetables are soft.

3. Meanwhile, trim off about 2 inches from the top of the large pumpkin and remove the seeds. The hollowed-out pumpkin will be used as a tureen for serving the soup.

4. When the soup is cooked, transfer to a food processor and process, in batches, until puréed. Return soup to the pot, taste and season with salt and pepper. If you find the soup too thick, adjust it with additional chicken stock.

5. Meanwhile, warm the inside of the pumpkin shell by pouring in enough boiling water to partially fill the cavity. Set aside for 3 to 5 minutes or until the shell is heated.

6. To finish the soup, pour in the brandy, stirring to combine. Transfer the soup to the pumpkin shell tureen. To serve, garnish individual servings with toasted hazelnuts.

Serves 10 to 12

Field Greens with Asian Dressing

In my days of flying, Tokyo was a regular route. Routinely after the flight a few of us would enjoy a light dinner and a glass of wine. Our very favorite salad was one prepared with soy sauce. The chef, however, refused to part with his recipe. So here is my rendition of the Narita Prince Soy Sauce Dressing. For the good old days!

Ingredients

Dressing

2   cloves garlic, minced

2   tablespoons Dijon mustard

2   tablespoons soy sauce

2   tablespoons rice vinegar

1   teaspoon freshly ground pepper

3/4 cup peanut oil

6 to 8 cups mixed baby greens, washed and patted dry

Method

1. Mix together the garlic, mustard, soy, vinegar and pepper. Slowly whisk in the oil, in a thin steady stream, continuing to whisk until the dressing is smooth and thick. Taste and adjust the seasoning.

2. Store in a glass jar or airtight container and set aside. (The dressing will keep for 2 weeks refrigerated.)

3. Toss the dressing together with the salad.

Serves 4 to 6

Creamy Garlic Dressing

This great all-purpose dressing can be made in minutes and will keep for 3 to 5 days in your refrigerator. I am particularly partial to Del Duca balsamic vinegar, which comes from Modena. The Groseli family, José and I have spent many wonderful evenings in Modena together. Through those times I have learned to completely appreciate their life's passion of creating one of the finest balsamic vinegars in Italy.

Ingredients

2   tablespoons Dijon mustard

2 or 3 cloves garlic

1   small egg

1   medium shallot, peeled

1/4 cup balsamic vinegar

1/2 teaspoon sea salt

1   teaspoon freshly ground pepper

1   cup extra virgin olive oil

Method

1. Place the mustard, garlic, egg, shallot, balsamic, salt and pepper in the bowl of a food processor fitted with a plastic blade. Process for 10 to 15 seconds until everything is pureéd, scraping down the sides of the bowl as needed.

2. With the motor running, pour in the olive oil, at first just a few drops at a time. Continue to pour in the oil, in a very slow, steady stream until blended. The dressing should emusify into a thick creamy consistency.

3. Chill for 1 hour before, then taste and adjust the seasonings.

Makes 11/2 cups

Pictured on page 33

 New Wave Nicoise

My contemporary version of the French classic calls for fresh tuna, rather than canned, as well as quail eggs.

The sharp and tangy dressing uses wasabi, the Japanese condiment made from dried horseradish.

Ingredients

1   pound young green beans, trimmed

1 1/2   pound fresh ahi or yellowfin tuna

   All-purpose flour, for dredging

3   tablespoons olive oil

Dressing

2   shallots, finely diced

1   clove garlic, minced

1/3   cup rice wine vinegar

1 to 2 teaspoons wasabi

2 to 3 tablespoons tequila

1   tablespoon soy sauce

1   cup peanut oil

   Sea salt

   Freshly ground pepper

1   cup French niçoise olives

1   green pepper, julienned

1   small purple onion, thinly sliced
     in rings

6   quail eggs, hard-cooked and peeled

12 to 15 cherry tomatoes

3   cups mixed lettuces

Method

1. Cook the beans in boiling water for 1 to 2 minutes until crisp tender. Drain and refresh in cold water to stop the cooking process. Set aside. Preheat oven to 375°.

2. Dredge the tuna in some flour, shaking off the excess. Heat some oil in a cast iron pan until hot. Add the tuna and pan-fry for about 4 minutes per side, turning once. Transfer pan to the oven and cook for about 10 minutes or until the tuna is cooked through but flakes. Set aside to cool.

DRESSING

3. For the dressing, combine the shallots, garlic, vinegar, wasabi, tequila and soy. Slowly whisk in to the oil until combined. Taste and adjust seasonings with salt and pepper.

4. Line a serving plate with mixed greens. Arrange the beans, olives, green pepper, onion, quail eggs and cherry tomatoes over the greens. Place the tuna on top and spoon the dressing just before serving.

Serves 6

 Light-Bodied Burgundy

Caesar Salad with Herbed Garlic Croutons

What could be more traditional than this classic Caesar salad served with homemade herbed croutons.

Ingredients

3	tablespoons olive oil
3	tablespoons unsalted butter
2	cups day-old French bread, cut into $^1/_4$-inch cubes
2	cloves garlic, minced
$^1/_2$	teaspoon dried oregano
$^1/_2$	teaspoon dried basil
$^1/_2$	teaspoon dried thyme
$^1/_2$	teaspoon dried savory
2	teaspoons minced fresh parsley
1	teaspoon sea salt
	Freshly ground pepper

Dressing

2	cloves garlic, chopped
1	teaspoon Worcestershire sauce
	Juice of $^1/_2$ a small lemon
1	tablespoon Dijon mustard
1	egg yolk
6	anchovy fillets
1	teaspoon freshly ground pepper
$^1/_2$	cup extra virgin olive oil
1	large head romaine lettuce, washed and dried
$^1/_2$	cup shaved Parmesan cheese

Method

1. To make croutons, heat the butter and oil in a heavy pan. When hot, add the cubed bread and cook for about 4 minutes. Add the garlic, oregano, basil, thyme, savory, parsley, salt and pepper, tossing well to coat the bread with the seasonings.

2. Reduce the heat and continue to cook until the bread is golden brown and crisp. Taste and adjust seasoning. Set aside (or store in an airtight container).

3. To make dressing, place the garlic, Worcestershire, lemon juice, Dijon, yolk, anchovies and pepper in the bowl of the food processor fitted with a metal blade. Pulse a few times, stopping to scrape down the sides of the bowl.

4. With the machine running, slowly pour in the oil in a thin, steady stream, until the dressing emulsifies and becomes smooth and creamy. Taste, adjust the seasonings and set aside.

5. Toss the salad greens with enough dressing to coat the leaves. Sprinkle the croutons on top and garnish with the shavings of Parmesan cheese.

serves 6

Celery Root Salad

There are very few ingredients I like that come from a can, but for this recipe canned celery root is superior to the fresh. Fresh celery root has a tendency to darken immediately after it is cut, but canned, which is packed in a saline solution, remains crisp and pure white.

Ingredients

Dressing:

1 garlic clove minced

1 tablespoon Dijon mustard

2 tablespoons rice wine vinegar

2 tablespoons soy sauce

$^2/_3$ cup peanut oil

1 teaspoon sea salt

1 teaspoon freshly ground pepper

3 cups celery root, rinsed, drained and julienned

$^1/_2$ sweet onion, thinly sliced

1 14-ounce jar roasted red peppers, drained and julienned

$^3/_4$ cup kalamata olives, pitted and chopped

$^1/_2$ pound fresh asparagus spears

$^1/_3$ bunch cilantro, chopped

Edible flowers, if available

Method

1. For the dressing, combine the garlic, mustard, vinegar and soy. Slowly whisk in the peanut oil in a thin, steady stream, continually whisking until the dressing smooth and thick. Season with salt and pepper and set aside.

2. Blanch the asparagus in boiling water for about 2 minutes. Remove and refresh in cold water to stop the cooking process. Drain and pat dry.

3. In a large bowl combine the celery root, onion, peppers, olives and asparagus.

4. Pour the dressing over the vegetables and toss well.

5. Mound the salad onto a serving platter, sprinkle the cilantro and decorate with fresh flowers, if available.

Serves 6

Beets and Chevre on Mixed greens

Soft, creamy chèvre complements cooked yet slightly firm beets in this rich-tasting salad of mixed baby greens.

A delicious champagne vinegar and walnut oil vinaigrette is spooned over the top.

Ingredients

1   head unpeeled garlic

2   large fresh beets

Dressing

1   tablespoon coarse-textured Dijon
    mustard

2   tablespoons champagne vinegar
    (or white wine vinegar)

1   teaspoon sea salt

2   teaspoons freshly ground pepper

2/3 cup walnut oil

6   ounces soft chevre

2   teaspoons freshly ground pepper

3   cups mixed greens (such as
    radicchio, arugula, endive, butter
    lettuce)

1/3 cup chopped walnuts, toasted

Method

1. For the garlic, preheat oven to 325°. Cut 1/4inch off the top of the garlic head and rub it all over with olive oil. Place in a garlic roaster or wrap loosely in foil. Bake for 45 minutes to an hour, depending on the size of the garlic. The garlic is done when it becomes soft and golden.

2. Meanwhile, boil the beets for 20 to 25 minutes until cooked through. When cool enough to handle, peel and cut into 1/4-inch-thick slices. Set aside.

3. Whisk together the mustard, vinegar, salt and pepper. Slowly pour in the oil in a thin, steady stream, whisking continuously until the dressing emulsifies and becomes smooth. Taste and adjust seasonings.

4. Squeeze half of the cooked garlic into a bowl (if you love garlic, use it all). Add the chèvre and pepper and mix well until smooth.

5. To assemble, toss the salad greens with the dressing and mound onto a salad plate. Spoon some cheese mixture on top of the beets and then arrange a few slices on top of the greens. Garnish with toasted walnuts to serve.

Serves 6

Spinach Salad in Bread Bowls

I developed this recipe for a television spot that I do on the Canadian Gardener Show with David Tarrant. His spinach was being harvested and he needed a recipe, so here is my version of Spinach Salad served in edible bread bowls.

Ingredients

Dough

1/2	cup warm water
1	teaspoon sugar
1	tablespoon dry yeast
4	cups unbleached all-purpose flour
2	tablespoons olive oil
1	teaspoon sea salt
1	cup water
6	ovenproof bowls (about 10-ounce size)

Method

DOUGH

1. For the bread, place the warm water in a bowl. Add the sugar, stirring to combine. Sprinkle the surface with yeast and let it rest for about 10 minutes or until the mixture begins to bubble.

2. Place the flour, olive oil, salt and proofed yeast into the bowl of a food processor fitted with a metal blade. Pulse 5 or 6 times to combine ingredients. Turn the machine on and with motor running, pour in the remaining 1 cup of water. Process until the dough becomes sticky and leaves the sides of the bowl.

3. Remove the dough and place in a lightly oiled bowl. (However if it is quite sticky, first knead in some additional flour until the dough becomes smooth and elastic.) Cover the bowl with a kitchen towel and place in a warm, draft-free area for 1 to 2 hours or until doubled in size.

4. Punch down the risen dough, turn out onto a lightly floured surface and cut into 6 equal pieces.

5. Lightly oil the outside of each ovenproof bowl and place them, upside down on a cookie sheet. Preheat the oven to 450°.

6. Roll each piece of dough into a circle about 6 inches in diameter or just large enough to fit over the bowls. Shape each circle of dough over the inverted bowls. Bake for 15 to 20 minutes or until the dough is golden. Remove the bowls and lower the oven temperature to 375°.

7. Carefully lift the breads off the bowls and return to the cookie sheet. Bake for about 10 minutes longer or until the inside of each bread bowl is no longer damp. Cool and and set aside.

Makes 6 bowls

Ingredients

Salad

$^1/_3$ cup sultana raisins

$^1/_4$ cup brandy

1   tablespoon olive oil

10   shiitake mushrooms, thinly sliced

12   strips Italian pancetta or bacon

2 or 3 bunches fresh young spinach,
   washed with stems removed

8   small button mushrooms, sliced

$^1/_2$ red onion, sliced into rings

$^1/_2$ cup pine nuts, toasted

Dressing

$^1/_3$ cup malt vinegar

1   teaspoon sugar

1   teaspoon Worcestershire sauce

$^2/_3$ cup olive oil

  Sea salt

  Freshly ground pepper

$^1/_2$ cup shaved Parmesan

Method

SALAD

8. For the salad, place the raisins in a small bowl, add brandy and set aside to soak until raisins are plump.

9. Meanwhile, heat the 1 tablespoon oil in a fry pan. When hot, add the shiitake mushrooms and sauté for 4 to 5 minutes or until golden. Remove and set aside. Chop the pancetta and sauté over medium heat for 4 to 5 minutes. Remove and set aside.

10. In a large bowl, combine the spinach, shiitakes, button mushrooms, onion, pine nuts and pancetta, tossing to combine Drain the raisins, reserving the brandy, and add them to the salad.

DRESSING

11. For the dressing, combine the reserved brandy, vinegar, sugar and Worcestershire. Slowly whisk in the olive oil. Taste and adjust the seasonings with the salt and pepper.

12. Pour dressing over the salad, tossing well to coat, and fill each bread bowl. Garnish with the Parmesan shavings.

Serves 6

Crisp Iceberg with Roasted Garlic Dressing

Oven-roasted garlic is the dominant flavor in the creamy dressing which is spooned over wedges of crisp iceberg lettuce.

A large head of iceberg usually serves 6 to 8 guests.

Ingredients

1   whole firm head of garlic

1   tablespoon olive oil

1   cup buttermilk

1/2   cup mayonnaise

1/2   teaspoon sea salt

1   teaspoon freshly ground pepper

3   tablespoons chopped fresh dill

1   large head iceburg lettuce

Fresh chives and sun-dried olives

Method

1. Cut 1/4 inch off the top of the garlic head. Rub the entire head with olive oil.

2. Place the garlic in a garlic roaster, or wrap it in foil, and bake in a 325° degree oven for 45 minutes to an hour, depending on the size of garlic. The garlic will be soft when completely roasted. Set aside to cool.

3. Whisk together the buttermilk, mayonnaise, salt, pepper and dill.

4. Separate the head of garlic into cloves and squeeze out the softened portion from each clove. Mash the pulp with the back of a spoon until smooth and then whisk into the mayonnaise mixture. Taste and adjust the seasonings. Cover and chill for at least 2 hours before serving.

5. Meanwhile, cut the iceberg into wedges. Arrange a wedge on each individual serving plate and ladle a generous spoon of the dressing over top. Garnish with a chive sprig and a few sun-dried olives.

Serves 6 to 8

Cress, Apple & Endive Salad

The fresh flavors of crisp watercress and Belgian endive combine beautifully in the salad made with tart apples and blue-veined cheese. If the endive are large, sliced them in half lengthwise.

Ingredients

Dressing

1	large shallot, minced
3	tablespoons champagne or sherry vinegar
1	teaspoon sea salt
1/2	teaspoon fresh ground pepper
3/4	cup walnut oil

Salad

3	bunches fresh watercress, washed with stems removed
3 or 4	heads Belgian endive
2	large Granny Smith apples, cored and thinly sliced
1	cup fresh button mushrooms, sliced
12	ounces creamy-style blue cheese
1/2	cup almonds, toasted

Method

1. Stir together the shallot, vinegar, salt and pepper. Slowly whisk in the walnut oil, in a thin, slow but steady stream, until the dressing emulsifies and becomes smooth. Taste and adjust seasonings.

2. In a large bowl, toss together the watercress, endive, apples and mushrooms.

3. Pour the dressing over the salad and toss well.

4. Place a portion of the salad on each plate. Scatter the cheese equally among the plates and garnish with the toasted almonds.

Serves 6

Northern Italian Bean Salad

This salad travels well. Take it to the cottage, on a picnic or to your pot luck. Leftovers taste even better so it's a good idea to make a double amount.

Ingredients

4	cups cooked white navy beans
1	14 ounce can or jar roasted red peppers
1/4	pound thinly sliced pancetta
1	medium yellow onion, diced
2 to 3	garlic cloves, minced
2	tablespoons Dijon mustard
1/4	cup balsamic vinegar
3/4	cup extra virgin olive oil
	Sea salt to taste
	Fresh ground pepper to taste
1	small head radicchio, for lining the plate

Method

1. Drain and blot the peppers, cut them into about 1/2-inch dice. Set aside.

2. Chop the pancetta up and fry it crisp. Drain on paper towels and set aside.

3. In a sauté pan, heat 1/4 cup of the olive oil, add the onion and garlic cooking until they are barely golden and soft, about 5-8 minutes. Turn off the heat. Whisk in the mustard and balsamic. Then, in a slow steady stream, whisk in the remaining oil adjusting the seasonings with the salt & pepper.

4. Pour the warm dressing over the cooked beans, toss in the peppers and mix to coat well. Line each individual plate with the radicchio and evenly spoon the bean mixture onto the leaves. Top with the crisp pancetta.

Serves 6 to 8

Rice & Black Bean Salad with Ancho Chili Dressing

Rice and beans are combined in this colorful salad to create a healthy alternative to traditional main course salads containing meat. The smoky flavor of ancho chilies goes nicely with the citrus and cilantro.

Ingredients

Salad

3	cups cooked long-grain rice
2	cups cooked black turtle beans
1	cup peeled and diced jicama
1	green pepper, seeded and diced
2	cups red seedless grapes
1	small mango, peeled and diced

Dressing

3	ancho chilies
2	large shallots, peeled and minced
2	cloves garlic, minced
$1/3$	cup chopped fresh cilantro
1 to 2	tablespoons Dijon mustard
1	teaspoon sea salt
2	teaspoons freshly ground pepper
$1/4$	cup fresh lemon juice or lime juice
$3/4$	cup peanut oil or corn oil

Method

1. Soak the ancho chilies in 2 cups of the hot water for about 20 minutes or until soft.

2. Drain the chilies and finely chop.

3. Transfer to a bowl and add the shallots, garlic, cilantro, mustard, salt, pepper and lemon juice, mixing to combine. Slowly whisk in the oil, a little at a time, until the dressing becomes thick.

4. In a large serving bowl combine the rice, black beans, jicama, green pepper, grapes and mango. Pour the dressing over the salad and toss to combine. Taste and adjust the seasonings as needed. Chill until serving.

Serves 6 to 8

Asian Vegetable & Noodle Salad with Ginger Dressing

Serve this multicolored spicy salad with any grilled fish, meat or poultry or by itself as a light entrée. The flavor of the salad improves tremendously if you chill it for a few hours before serving.

Ingredients

Salad

1	pound fresh Chinese noodles
$1/2$	pound fresh asparagus, trimmed
$1/2$	pound fresh snow peas
1	red pepper, seeded and julienned
1	yellow pepper, seeded and julienned
1	large carrot, peeled and thinly sliced
1	cup water chestnuts, sliced
1	bunch green onions, chopped
$1/2$	cup chopped fresh cilantro
$1/3$	cup toasted sesame seeds

Dressing

1	tablespoon rice wine vinegar
$2/3$	cup mayonnaise
1	tablespoon minced fresh ginger
1	tablespoon dry hot mustard powder
$1/2$	cup soy sauce
$1/3$	cup sesame oil
$1/3$	cup peanut oil
1 to 2	tablespoons hot chili flakes

Method

1. Cook the noodles in plenty of boiling salted water for 3 to 5 minutes or until just cooked. Rinse them well with cold running water, drain and set aside.

2. Blanch asparagus in boiling water for 2 minutes. Refresh in cold water to protect their color and stop the cooking process, blot dry and set aside.

3. String the snow peas and blanch them in boiling salted water for only 10 to 15 seconds. Refresh them in cold water, blot dry and set aside.

4. For the dressing, whisk together the vinegar, mayonnaise, ginger, mustard, soy, sesame oil, and peanut oil. Add the chili flakes, adjusting the amount to suit your taste. Pour the dressing over the noodles and toss well.

5. Add the red and yellow peppers, carrot, water chestnuts, onion, asparagus and cilantro. Toss just enough to distribute the vegetables evenly. (I find it easiest to mix the salad with my hands.)

6. Line a serving platter with the reserved snow peas. Mound the noodle and vegetable mixture in the center and garnish with toasted sesame seeds.

Serves 6 to 8

Cold Duck Pasta Salad

Full of flavor, this spectacular salad makes quite an impression on the buffet table. The real beauty, though,

is in the preparation. I buy the duck from a local Chinese restaurant and the pasta —I like Al Dente brand--cooks in just minutes.

Ingredients

8   dried Chinese mushrooms

Dressing

2   cloves garlic, minced

1   piece (about $^1/_2$ inch) fresh
     ginger, minced

$^1/_2$ to $^3/_4$ cup peanut oil

1   tablespoon fish sauce

2   tablespoons rice wine vinegar

$^1/_4$ cup soy sauce

1   teaspoon hot chili flakes

1 to 2 tablespoons sesame oil

$^3/_4$ cup chopped cilantro

Salad

1   pound snow peas, trimmed

18 ounces spicy sesame pasta
     (or other spicy dried pasta)

1   purchased Chinese barbecued duck
     (about 2 to 3 pounds)

$^1/_4$ cup snipped chives (or sliced green
     onion tops)

$^1/_2$ cup slivered almonds, toasted

$^1/_4$ cup black sesame seeds, toasted

Method

1. Place the dried mushrooms in a bowl and add enough boiling water to cover. Set aside to soak for about 20 minutes.

2. For the dressing, combine the garlic, ginger, peanut oil, fish sauce, vinegar, soy chili flakes, sesame oil and cilantro. Set aside.

3. Blanch the snow peas in boiling water for about 3 minutes. Drain and refresh immediately in cold water; then blot dry and set aside.

4. Cook the pasta in plenty of boiling salted water until al dente. Drain and toss in a large bowl with 1 to 2 tablespoons oil, to prevent sticking. Set aside.

5. Meanwhile, drain the mushrooms; cut off and discard the woody stems. Julienne the mushrooms and add to the pasta. Pour the dressing over the pasta, tossing to combine.

6. Remove all the meat from the duck, discarding the skin, fat and bones. Shred the meat and add to the pasta along with the chives. Taste and adjust seasonings.

7. To serve, line a decorative platter with snow peas and mound the pasta in the center. Garnish with almonds and black sesame seeds.

Serves 6 to 8

Roasted Chicken Salad with Tropical Salsa

The spicy flavors of chili powder, cumin and garlic turn ordinary chicken breasts into something special,

especially when served on a bed of radicchio accompanied by a colorful, fresh-tasting salsa.

Ingredients

Chicken

2	cloves garlic, minced
1/4	cup extra virgin olive oil
1	tablespoon freshly ground pepper
1	teaspoon ground cumin
1	tablespoon pure chili powder
4	whole boneless chicken breasts, skin removed

Salsa

2	ripe avocados
1	ripe papaya
2	cloves garlic, minced
1/4	medium purple onion, finely chopped
2	large roma tomatoes, chopped
	Juice of 1/2 fresh lemon
1	teaspoon piri piri sauce or Tabasco
	Sea salt
	Freshly ground pepper
1	head radicchio, washed and dried

Method

CHICKEN

1. Preheat the oven to 375°. Combine the garlic, oil, pepper, cumin and chili powder, stirring together to make a paste. Gently lift up the skin from the chicken breast and rub the paste directly onto the meat. Repeat on the other breast.

2. Place the chicken in a roasting pan and bake for about 45 minutes, taking care not to overbake or the chicken will become tough.

3. When the chicken is done, remove from the oven and set aside to cool.

SALSA

4. Meanwhile, to make salsa, peel, pit and coarsely chop the avocados and the papaya, placing the flesh into a bowl. Add the garlic, onion, tomatoes, lemon juice, and piri piri, stirring to combine. Taste and adjust seasonings with salt and pepper.

5. To serve, arrange the radicchio on a serving platter. Slice the chicken breasts lengthwise and arrange on the radicchio. Spoon the salsa into the center.

Serves 6

 Sagres Beer

Breads, Pizza & Pasta

Classic Focaccia

Sun-dried Tomato Bread

Olive-Basil Bread

Muffuletta

Fresh Artichoke Pizza

Gorgonzola & Pine Nut Pizza

Roasted Chicken with Brie Pizza

Mini Calzones

Asian Pasta with Black Sesame Seeds

Mixed Mushroom Pasta

Pasta Primavera

Penne Puttanesca

Orecchiette with Sun-dried Tomato Pesto

Black Pasta with Smoked Salmon

Shrimp-filled Wonton Ravioli with Saffron Sauce

Farfalle with Italian Sausage & Radicchio

Hearty Vegetable Lasagna

Gnocchi with Classic Italian Sauce

Roasted Chicken Lasagna with Wild Mushrooms

Creamy Polenta with Wild Mushrooms

Grilled Polenta with Summer Ratatouille

Risotto with Fennel

Risotto Croquettes

Wild Rice with Sultana Raisins & Shiitake Mushrooms

# Classic Focaccia

Focaccia often is baked with a little olive oil, sea salt and sprinkling of fresh rosemary.

However, I prefer to knead chopped rosemary directly into the dough, either by machine or by hand, and then brush it liberally with

extra virgin olive oil and top it with coarse sea salt and more rosemary.

Ingredients

1	tablespoon dry yeast
1	teaspoon granulated sugar
1 $^3/_4$	cups warm water
1	teaspoon sea salt
2	tablespoons extra virgin olive oil
4 $^1/_2$ to 5	cups unbleached all-purpose flour
4	tablespoons fresh rosemary, chopped
1 to 2	tablespoons coarse sea salt
	Extra olive oil, for brushing

Method

1. Place 3/4 cup of the warm water in a bowl. Add the sugar, stirring to combine. Sprinkle the surface with the yeast and let it rest for about 10 minutes or until the mixture begins to bubble.

2. Place the remaining 1 cup of water, 2 tablespoons olive oil and the salt in a large mixing bowl of a heavy-duty mixer that is fitted with a dough hook. Add the proofed yeast, 2 tablespoons of the rosemary, and the flour 1 cup at a time. Slowly beat to incorporate until the dough comes together in a smooth elastic mass. (Alternatively you can knead the dough by hand, on a floured surface, for 3 to 5 minutes.)

3. Place the dough in a lightly oiled bowl, cover with a kitchen towel and place in a warm, draft-free location until doubled in size.

4. Punch down the dough, turn out and press evenly into a large, lightly-oiled cookie sheet with 1-inch sides.

5. Prick the dough all over with a fork, brush generously with additional olive oil and sprinkle with the coarse sea salt and remaining rosemary. Let the dough rise for 30 minutes.

6. Preheat oven to 400°. Bake the focaccia for 20 minutes or until browned. Brush top surface with additional olive oil, cut into pieces and serve warm.

Serves 6 to 8

Sun-dried Tomato Bread

The great thing about this basic bread recipe is that it's so versatile. As a variation, add pan-roasted shallots and diced Swiss cheese instead of the tomatoes, or a tablespoon of herbes de Provence. You'll need a 4 1/2-inch x 8 1/2-inch loaf pan for baking.

Ingredients

Bread

1	tablespoon dry yeast
1	teaspoon granulated sugar
$1/4$	cup milk
$3/4$	cup sun-dried tomatoes
2	cups unbleached all-purpose flour
3	eggs, beaten
$1/4$	teaspoon ground white pepper
$1/4$	cup unsalted butter, room temperature
	Additional all-purpose flour, for kneading

Glaze

1	egg
$1/2$	teaspoon salt

Method

BREAD

1. Heat the milk and sugar together until lukewarm. Sprinkle the yeast over the milk and set aside for about 10 minutes until it begins to bubble.

2. Meanwhile, soak the tomatoes in enough hot water to cover for about 10 minutes. Drain and set aside.

3. Chop the tomatoes. Sift the flour, salt and pepper directly onto a board or suitable work surface. Stir in the tomatoes, making sure that each piece is well coated with flour.

4. Gather up the flour mixture into a pile and make a well in the center. Add the eggs and proofed yeast. Gradually draw in the flour, working with your hands, to form a soft dough. Knead spoonfuls of butter into the dough, continuing to knead for about 5 minutes longer or until the dough becomes smooth and elastic. While kneading, keep the board well floured so that the dough doesn't stick.

5. Place the dough in a lightly buttered bowl, rolling it around so that the top is also buttered. Cover with a kitchen towel and let rise in a warm, draft-free location for about an hour or until doubled in size.

6. Turn out the dough and punch it down. Shape and place in a greased bread pan and let it rise for about 30 minutes more.

GLAZE

7. Meanwhile, preheat oven to 375°. Combine the egg and the salt. Brush the top of the bread with the glaze. Bake for 35 to 45 minutes or until golden. To test for doneness, listen for a hollow sound when tapping the bottom of the loaf.

Makes 1 loaf

 **live-Basil Bread**

This bread is baked on a sheet the same way as focaccia. I let it rise so it is nice and thick.

The flavors are intense with plenty of chopped kalamata olives and fresh basil. This bread brings standing ovations, I guarantee it!

Ingredients

2   cups warm water

2   teaspoons sugar

1   tablespoon dry yeast

5   cups unbleached all purpose flour

3   teaspoons sea salt

1 $^1/_4$ cups kalamata olives ,pitted, chopped

$^1/_2$ cup fresh basil leaves

3   tablespoons olive oil

   Olive oil, for brushing

2   teaspoons coarse sea salt

Method

1. Measure and pour 1/2 cup of the warm water into a bowl. Add the sugar, stirring to combine. Sprinkle the surface with yeast and let it rest for about 10 minutes or until the mixture begins to bubble.

2. Place the 5 cups of flour in the large bowl of a heavy-duty mixer fitted with the dough hook. Add the proofed yeast along with 1 teaspoon of the salt. Stir in the remaining 1 1/2 cups warm water, olives, basil and oil. Let the machine run, stopping at intervals to scrape down the side of the bowl, until well blended.

3. Place the dough in an oiled bowl, cover with a kitchen towel and let it rise in a warm, draft-free location, for about an hour or until doubled in size.

4. Oil a cookie sheet with 1-inch sides. Spread the dough out onto the cookie sheet, cover with a kitchen towel and set aside in a warm location for about an hour or until doubled in size.

5. Preheat oven to 400° Brush the top of the dough lightly with olive oil and sprinkle with the 2 remaining teaspoons of coarse sea salt. Bake for 15 to 20 minutes or until golden brown. Cut into squares and serve warm.

Serves 8

# Muffuletta

A muffultta is actually layers of different cheeses and meats compressed together between a flavorful olive marinade. It takes a little time to chop and pit the olives, but every minute spent is more than made up with the impact of taste. I love taking this on picnics or boating. It's all you need . . . well . . . except for wine of course.

Ingredients

1   large round loaf of Italian bread, about 12 inches in diameter

Filling

1 1/2   cups pimento-stuffed green olives, sliced

1/3   cup minced parsley

1   cup Greek olives, pitted, chopped

2 or 3 anchovy fillets, mashed

3   tablespoons capers

2   cloves garlic, minced

2   teaspoons dried Greek oregano

1   cup roasted red peppers, drained and chopped

2/3   cup olive oil

Freshly ground pepper

1   teaspoon dried basil

1/4   pound Genoa salami or other hard salami, sliced

1/4   pound mortadella, sliced

1/4   pound provolone cheese or fontina, sliced

1/4   pound Swiss or mozzarella, sliced

Method

1. In a large bowl, combine the green olives, parsley, Greek olives, anchovies, capers, garlic, oregano, peppers, oil, salt and pepper. Mix well, cover and refrigerate for at least 2 hours.

2. Meanwhile, slice the loaf of bread in half horizontally. Pull out most of the dough in the center, leaving about a 1/2-inch edge all around. Brush the inside of the bread shell with some of the oil in the olive mixture.

3. Using a slotted spoon, scoop out 1/2 of the olive mixture and spread it evenly into the bottom of the bread shell. Press in evenly.

4. Alternate slices of meats and cheeses over top, stacking them as you go, and then spoon the remaining drained olive mixture on top.

5. Place the bread lid back on top and wrap the entire loaf tightly in plastic wrap. Place the wrapped loaf in a large pot and top with a 3 to 4-pound weight. (I often use a large pot filled with canned goods.) This compresses the sandwich and makes it dense.

6. Chill for at least 30 minutes, then unwrap and slice into wedges.

Serves 6 to 8

Chianti Classico, such as Salcetino

 resh Artichoke Pizza

I have used fresh baby artichokes for this pizza, however if they are not available in your area, use the large ones and cut them up or simply substitute the canned variety. This pizza is great any way.

Ingredients

Basic Dough

1/2	cup warm water
1	teaspoon sugar
1	tablespoon dry yeast
3	cups unbleached flour
2	teaspoons sea salt
1	teaspoon chopped fresh rosemary
1	teaspoon chopped fresh thyme
3	tablespoons extra virgin olive oil
3/4	cup warm water

Topping

15 to 20 fresh baby artichokes, cooked and halved

1 cup tomato sauce

4 to 5 balls of fresh mozzarella cheese (bocconcini)

1 large red pepper, julienned

3/4 cup sun-dried tomatoes, chopped

1/2 pound pancetta, sliced thin

1/2 cup freshly grated Parmesan cheese

1 cup fresh basil leaves , for garnish

Method

BASIC DOUGH

1. Dissolve the sugar in the 1/2 cup of warm water, sprinkle the yeast on top and let it proof (bubble) about 5 minutes.

2. Place the flour, salt, rosemary and thyme in the bowl of a food processor; add the oil, proofed yeast and the 3/4 cup of warm water. Pulse the machine a few times, then let it run until the dough forms a ball at the side of the bowl, about 1 minute.

3. Remove the dough to a floured work surface and knead it for about 2 minutes. Rub the top of the dough with a little olive oil, cover and let it rest for 1 hour or until doubled. Turn the dough out onto a cookie sheet and dress with any combination of ingredients.

TOPPING

4. Preheat the oven to 425°. Lightly brush the pizza dough with the tomato sauce. Evenly distribute the artichokes, mozzarella, red pepper and tomatoes, leaving the pancetta until last so that it will cook crisp. Sprinkle on the Parmesan cheese and bake for about 15 to 20 minutes or until the cheese bubbles and the crust is brown.

5. Remove the pizza from the oven, brush the edges of the dough with a little olive oil and sprinkle the basil leaves over top. Cut into squares and serve at once.

P.S. Cold pizza tastes great for breakfast!

Serves 6

Your favorite beer

Gorgonzola and Pine Nut Pizza

Although the ingredient list for this pizza is not extensive, don't let it deceive you. The intense flavor of the Gorgonzola spreads its wealth of taste throughout the pizza, requiring just a sprinkle of pine nuts and fresh basil to complete this unique taste.

Ingredients

Basic Dough

see page 60 for basic dough recipe

$1/4$ cup extra virgin olive oil

$1/2$ cup freshly grated Parmesan cheese

8 to 10 ounces Italian Gorgonzola cheese

1   cup European pine nuts, toasted

1   cup fresh basil leaves

    Freshly ground pepper

Method

1. Preheat the oven to 425°.

2. Lightly oil a cookie sheet, spread the dough evenly over the pan. Brush the dough evenly with the 1/4 cup of oil, sprinkle with the Parmesan cheese.

3. Remove any dark rind from the Gorgonzola. Crumble the cheese evenly over the pizza. If you like a thick crust pizza, leave it to rise for 30 to 40 minutes. If you prefer a thinner crust, place it in the oven now. Bake for 15 to 20 minutes or until the edges of the dough are browned.

4. Remove from the oven, brush the edges lightly with olive oil. Sprinkle the pine nuts over top and garnish with the chopped fresh basil.

5. Cut into squares and serve immediately.

Serves 6

 Your favorite beer

Roasted Chicken Pizza with Brie

A pizza crust can be transformed into almost anything. In this version of pizza we are using cooked chicken,

sliced mushrooms and a creamy Brie. No, we didn't forget the tomato sauce. The flavor is intensified without the standard

red sauce. It's a great way to use last night's leftover chicken.

Ingredients

Basic Dough

See page 60 for basic dough recipe

Topping

$1/3$	cup extra virgin olive oil
$1/2$	cup freshly grated Parmesan cheese
3	cups slivered roasted chicken
2	cups fresh button mushrooms, sliced
$1/2$	pound Brie or Camembert
$1/2$	cup chopped walnuts, toasted

Method

1. Lightly oil a cookie sheet. Turn the dough out onto the pan, spreading it evenly. Brush the dough with olive oil and sprinkle with Parmesan cheese.

2. Remove the outer rind from the Brie and slice about 1/4-inch thick. Set aside.

3. Arrange the chicken meat over the dough, evenly distribute the mushrooms and Brie.

4. Preheat the oven to 425°. If you like a thick-crust pizza, let the pizza sit for 30 minutes before baking it. This will allow the dough to rise again creating a thicker crust.

5. To serve, lightly brush the edges of the dough with olive oil, sprinkle with the chopped walnuts, cut into squares and serve hot.

Serves 6

 Your favorite beer

Mini Calzone

Really, a little pizza folded in half with all or nothing inside. It's up to you to be extravagant or frugal. A basic pizza dough, rolled, filled and baked. I'm not an enthusiast of freezing anything, however, these do freeze well for an emergency.

Ingredients

Dough

$1/2$	cup warm water
1	teaspoon sugar
1	package yeast
1	teaspoon sea salt
3	cups flour
3	tablespoons olive oil
$3/4$	cup additional water

Filling

3	tablespoons olive oil
1	large onion, sliced
2	cloves garlic, mashed
1	teaspoon dried basil
1	teaspoon dried oregano
1	teaspoon freshly ground pepper
$1/2$	cup Jarlsberg cheese, cut into small cubes
1	egg, lightly beaten, for wash

Method

1. Combine the water and the sugar in a bowl. Sprinkle the yeast over the water and set aside for about 10 minutes or until it begins to bubble.

2. Place the salt, flour and proofed yeast in a food processor fitted with a metal blade. With the motor running, slowly add the water and process until a ball of dough is formed and leaves the side of the bowl. If it is too sticky, add a bit more flour. Likewise, if it is too dry, add a bit more water.

3. Remove the dough and knead for about 10 minutes until smooth and elastic. Place in a bowl coated with olive oil, cover with a kitchen towel, and set aside in a warm, draft-free location for about an hour until doubled in size.

4. Meanwhile, for the filling, heat the oil in a frying pan. When the oil is hot, add the onion and garlic and cook over medium heat for 3 to 5 minutes or until onions begin to caramelize. Add the basil, oregano and pepper. Continue to cook, stirring occasionally, for about 15 minutes longer. Set aside to cool.

5. Punch the dough down and roll it out quite thinly on a light-floured board. Using a 3-inch cutter, cut out circles of dough.

6. Add the cheese to the cooled filling, stirring to combine. Spoon about 1 tablespoon filling on one half of each circle. Brush the edges with egg wash and fold in half, pressing the edges firmly together. Brush the tops with egg wash, transfer to a baking sheet and set aside for 20 minutes to rise briefly. Preheat the oven to 400°.

7. Bake the calzone for about 10 minutes or until golden.

Makes 12

 Your favorite beer or Californian Chardonnay

Asian Pasta with Black Sesame Seeds

My version of Asian pasta is prepared with a spicy sesame pasta. You may use the Chinese egg noodles instead.

To turn this dish into a more substantial meal, add some cooked shredded chicken or prawns.

Ingredients

$^1/_2$ pound snow peas

4   medium carrots, sliced thin

6   water chestnuts, sliced (preferably fresh ones)

$^1/_2$ cup peanut oil

1   bunch green onions, chopped fine

3   garlic cloves, minced

1   1-inch piece of fresh ginger, peeled & minced

3 to 4 tablespoons Thai chili sauce

2   tablespoons fish sauce

4   tablespoons pure sesame oil

$^1/_2$ cup soy sauce

$^1/_2$ pound fresh button mushrooms, sliced

1   red pepper, julienned

2   tablespoons cornstarch

$^1/_2$ cup water

1   12-ounce package Chinese egg noodles or *Al Dente Spicy Sesame Pasta*, cooked and drained

$^1/_2$ cup chopped fresh cilantro

3   tablespoons toasted black sesame seeds

Method

1. Blanch the carrots and snow peas in boiling water for about 3 minutes, refresh in ice water, blot dry and set aside.

2. Heat the peanut oil in a deep fry pan or wok. Add the onions, garlic, ginger, chili sauce, sesame oil and soy sauce. Cook until the sauce becomes fragrant, about 2 to 3 minutes. Add the mushrooms and peppers, continuing to cook for an additional 2 minutes.

3. Stir the cornstarch into the water, then whisk the mixture into the simmering sauce, continuing until the sauce is slightly thick.

4. Toss in the cooked pasta together with the sauce, reserved vegetables and cilantro. Pile high on a colorful serving platter and garnish with toasted black sesame seeds.

Serves 6

 Gewurtztraminer

Mixed Mushroom Pasta

I like the combination of fresh and dried mushrooms . This recipe takes the idea one step further by calling for wild mushroom pasta too, which is available at some markets and speciality shops.

Ingredients

$1/2$	cup dried wild mushrooms, such as cèpes, boletus or porcini
1	cup dry white wine
3	tablespoons unsalted butter
4	shallots, finely chopped
2	cloves garlic, minced
1	cup fresh mushrooms, sliced
1	teaspoon undiluted chicken bouillon powder
1	cup heavy cream
1	teaspoon sea salt
1	teaspoon freshly ground pepper
1	12 -ounce package wild mushroom pasta
$1/4$	bunch parsley, finely chopped
	Freshly grated Parmesan cheese

Method

1. Place the dried mushrooms in a bowl and cover with the white wine. Set them aside to soak for about 1 hour. The longer they soak the more intense the flavor becomes.

2. Meanwhile, melt the butter in a heavy-bottomed saucepan over medium heat. Add the shallots and let them sweat for about 2 minutes. Add the garlic and cook just until they both become soft but not brown.

3. Add the sliced fresh mushrooms and cook for another 3 minutes, stirring occasionally.

4. Drain the dried mushrooms, reserving the soaking wine, and pour through a coffee filter to catch any sand or grit that may have been on the mushrooms. Chop the mushrooms and add them to the pan of vegetables.

5. Pour in the cream and undiluted chicken bouillon powder. Reduce the heat and simmer for about 10 minutes or until the sauce is thick enough to coat the back of a spoon.

6. Add the strained reserved wine little by little as the sauce thickens to give it a nice flavor. (You will not need it all.) Taste and adjust seasonings.

7. Meanwhile, cook the pasta for about 3 to 5 minutes until al dente. Drain and place on a serving platter. Pour the sauce over the top and sprinkle with grated cheese and parsley to serve.

Serves 4 to 6

 Merryvale Sauvignon Blanc

Pasta Primavera

This pasta is always a favorite. I prepare it whenever I see loads of fresh vegetables in the market. I have given you an outline, but you can use whatever vegetables are available and of course freshest. If you cannot get the baby artichokes, use the big ones.

Ingredients

10	baby artichokes, or one 14-ounce tin, drained & quartered
2	tablespoons white vinegar
12 to 15	fresh asparagus spears
1	cup snap peas
3	young carrots, julienned
1/3	cup virgin olive oil
1	medium white onion, sliced
2	garlic cloves, minced
1/2	pound fresh button mushrooms, quartered
10	ripe Roma tomatoes, diced
3	tablespoons balsamic vinegar
1	cup red wine
2	teaspoons fresh thyme
2	teaspoons fresh oregano
1	sprig fresh sage
1	cup crushed tomatoes including liquid
1	red pepper julienned
	Sea salt
	Fresh ground pepper
3/4	cup fresh basil, chopped
	Fresh shavings of Parmesan cheese
1	12-ounce bag *Al Dente Garlic & Parsley Pasta*, cooked or
1	pound penne (or other fancy-shaped pasta), cooked

Method

1. Peel the outer leaves from the artichokes and trim the bottom. Plunge the artichokes into boiling water to which you add the vinegar to prevent discoloring. Boil them for about 8 to 10 minutes. Refresh in cold water, drain and cut them in half. Set aside.

2. Blanch the asparagus, snap peas and carrots in boiling water for about 2 minutes. Refresh in cold water, drain and set aside.

3. Heat the olive oil in a deep sauté pan, add the onion and garlic, cook the onion to light golden. Add the mushrooms, tomatoes, vinegar and wine. Simmer until the tomatoes are soft. Add the thyme, oregano, sage, crushed tomatoes, red pepper, salt and pepper to taste. Simmer the sauce for about 10 minutes. If you like a thicker sauce add more tomatoes. Alternatively, if you like it thinner, add more wine or a little stock or water.

4. Cook the pasta, drain well, toss it with about 2 tablespoons of olive oil to prevent the noodles from sticking together. Pour the warm sauce over the noodles, tossing well to coat the noodles evenly. In the same pan, quickly add the reserved vegetables, turn the heat to high and warm them through for about 30 seconds. Place the noodles on a large serving dish and top with the vegetables. Garnish with the basil and Parmesan cheese shavings.

Serves 6

Barbera

Penne Puttanesca

My editor refuses to let me divulge the original derivation of this Italian recipe, however I will say that the flavor of this pasta dish is based on the salty, spicy and hot tastes found in Southern Italy.

Ingredients

Sauce

$1/2$	cup olive oil
$1/2$	bunch green onions, chopped
1	small yellow onion, diced
3	cloves garlic, minced
4	anchovy fillets, chopped
3	tablespoons capers
1	cup kalamata olives, pitted and chopped
1 to 2	tablespoons hot chili flakes
2	cups crushed tomatoes
1	teaspoon sea salt
$1/2$	teaspoon freshly ground pepper
$1/2$	bunch basil, chopped
2	tablespoons minced parsley
	Freshly grated Parmesan cheese
1	pound cooked penne noodles

Method

1. Heat the olive oil in a large sauté pan. When oil is hot, add onions and garlic and cook for about 5 minutes or until soft. Stir in the anchovies and sauté for about 4 minutes longer or until they are almost dissolved.

2. Add the capers, olives, chili flakes and tomatoes. Reduce heat and simmer for 10 to 15 minutes or until the tomatoes begin to form a nice thick sauce. Stir in the basil, salt and pepper. Taste and adjust the seasonings.

3. To serve, toss the sauce with the hot cooked penne and garnish with minced parsley. Pass the fresh Parmesan at the table.

Serves 6

 Chianti Classico Salcetino

Orecchiette with Sun-dried Tomato Pesto

Nothing could be easier or more flavorful than this quick alternative to traditional basil pesto.

It is important to use Italian sun-dried tomatoes that are thick and fleshy because they will yield a richer pesto.

Ingredients

1	cup sun-dried tomatoes
3	large peeled garlic cloves
$^1/_3$	cup whole almonds
$^1/_3$	cup pine nuts
$^1/_2$	cup grated fresh Parmesan cheese
1	tablespoon ground five-blend peppercorns
1	teaspoon sea salt
$^3/_4$	cup extra virgin olive oil
1	pound orecchiette (or other fancy-shaped pasta), cooked

Method

1. Place the tomatoes in a bowl and cover them with hot water. Let them soak for 30 minutes. Drain well and place in the food processor fitted with a metal blade. Add the garlic and process until puréed.

2. Add the almonds and the pinenuts, Parmesan, pepper and salt. Process again, scraping down the sides of the bowl as needed, until smooth.

3. With the machine running, slowly pour in the oil in a thin steady stream until you have a smooth purée. The amount of oil determines how thick your pesto will be.

4. Taste and adjust seasonings with salt and pepper.

5. To serve, toss the pesto with the hot cooked pasta.

Serves 6

 Semillon

Asian Pasta with Black Sesame Seeds (page 64)

Shrimp Filled Wonton Ravioli with Saffron Sauce (page 74)

Fresh Artichoke Pizza (page 60)

Smoked Salmon with Black Pasta (page 73)

 Smoked Salmon with Black Pasta

The dramatic black of the pasta not only is beautiful to look at but equally delicious to eat. Use pasta that is colored with squid ink (no it doesn't taste fishy); it is natural and flavorless, but will not boil out of the pasta as it cooks. Black pasta made with food coloring will leave your water black and the pasta grey. I have chosen caperberries to accent the smoked salmon. The flavors are magic.

Ingredients

1   12-ounce package black pasta

³/₄   cup olive oil

2   shallots, finely chopped

1   bunch green onions, finely chopped

¹/₂   pound smoked salmon, flaked into small pieces

1 ¹/₂ teaspoons herbes de Provence

¹/₃   cup caperberries

1   teaspoon ground five-blend peppercorns

¹/₂   bunch cilantro, chopped

Method

1. Cook the pasta according to package directions until al dente.

2. Meanwhile, heat 1/4 cup of the oil in a large sauté pan. When the oil is hot, add the shallots and green onions and sauté for about 3 minutes or until softened. Take care not to let the onions brown.

3. When the pasta is cooked, drain well and toss it into the pan with the onions.

4. Add the remaining oil, salmon, herbes de Provence, most of the caperberries and pepper mixture. Toss well to distribute the ingredients evenly.

5. Transfer to a serving platter and garnish with the cilantro and a few extra caperberries. Serve hot.

Serves 4 to 6

 Pinot Grigio

Shrimp-filled Wonton Ravioli with Saffon Sauce

Making homemade ravioli is simplified by using very thin wonton wrappers instead of sheets of pasta. I used a

canapé cutter to create the oval, scalloped shape seen in the photograph.

Ingredients

Filling

- ¹/₂ pound cooked shrimp meat
- ¹/₂ cup ricotta cheese
- 1 teaspoon sea salt
- ¹/₂ teaspoon freshly ground white pepper
- 1 egg white
- 1 tablespoon finely minced green onion (white part only)
- 1 tablespoon finely minced red pepper
- ¹/₂ teaspoon piri piri sauce

- 1 8 oz package of wonton wrappers

Sauce

- 2 tablespoons unsalted butter
- 1 to 2 cloves garlic, minced
- 2 medium shallots, peeled and finely chopped
- ¹/₂ cup fish stock
- 1 teaspoon salt
- 1 teaspoon Spanish saffron threads
- ³/₄ cup heavy cream

Additional finely minced red pepper

Additional thinly sliced green onion

Whole cooked prawns, for garnish

Method

1. For the filling, finely chop the shrimp meat and place in a bowl. Add the ricotta cheese, salt, pepper, egg white, green onion, red pepper and piri piri, stirring to combine.

2. To make ravioli, lay a wonton wrapper on a lightly floured surface. Place a tablespoon or so of the prepared filling onto the middle of the wonton. Brush the edges liberally with water, place another wrapper on top and press edges well to seal. Repeat until all the filling is used, making sure you dust the filled ravioli with flour to prevent them from sticking to each other.

3. For a more decorative shape (as shown in the photograph), trim the ravioli using a canapé cutter. Chill (or cover and freeze) until ready to cook.

SAUCE

4. For the sauce, melt the butter in a saucepan. Add the garlic and the shallots and lightly sauté for about 2 minutes. Add the fish stock, bring to a boil and cook over medium heat until liquid is reduced by half.

5. Place the sea salt and the saffron in a mortar. Grind them together with the pestle until the saffron threads are powder. Stir into the sauce, add the heavy cream and let the sauce simmer until it is thick enough to coat the back of a spoon. Place a piece of waxed paper directly onto the sauce to prevent a skin from forming and set aside when cooking ravioli.

6. Meanwhile, cook the ravioli in plenty of boiling water, in batches, for 2 to 3 minutes or until they rise to the surface. Remove with a slotted spoon and keep warm.

7. To serve, spoon some warm sauce onto a dinner plate. Arrange a few ravioli on the sauce and garnish with a sprinkling of additional green onion, minced red pepper and a whole cooked prawn.
Serves 6 to 8

 White Bordeaux from France

Farfalle with Italian Sausage & Radicchio

On a recent culinary tour to Napa, my students and I tasted this unusual pasta at one of the wineries. Everyone loved it so much that I created a Northwest version using radicchio which is finished with a gratinée of cheese.

Ingredients

- 1/3 cup olive oil
- 1 medium yellow onion, diced
- 2 shallots, chopped
- 3 cloves garlic, minced
- 1 pound fresh Italian sausage
- 1 serrano chili diced (optional)
- 1 sprig (about 2 inches) fresh sage
- 2 teaspoons dried basil
- 2 teaspoons herbes de Provence
- 1 bay leaf
- 3 cups canned tomatoes, crushed
- 1/2 cup dry red wine
- 1/2 head radicchio, chopped
- 1/2 cup sun-dried tomatoes, chopped
- 1/4 cup capers
- 2/3 cup Greek olives, pitted
- Sea salt
- Coarsely ground pepper
- 1/4 pound mozzarella cheese, grated
- 1/4 pound Swiss cheese, grated

- 1 pound farfalle (bow tie pasta), cooked
- 1/4 bunch parsley, minced

Method

1. Heat the oil in a large sauté pan. When the oil is hot, add the onion, shallots and garlic and cook for about 5 minutes, taking care not to let them brown.

2. Remove the sausage from the casing and add to the pan. Fry until the sausage becomes brown and crumbled.

3. Stir in the chili, sage, basil, herbes de Provence and bay leaf. Pour in the tomatoes, reduce the heat and let the sauce simmer for about 30 minutes. Add the wine as the sauce reduces, a little at a time.

4. Add the radicchio, sun-dried tomatoes, capers and olives. Stir over medium heat for about 8 minutes or until the radicchio becomes wilted. Taste and adjust the seasonings with salt and pepper.

5. Toss the sauce with the cooked pasta, distributing the ingredients evenly. Spoon into a large oven-proof gratin dish (or individual dishes) and top with the grated cheeses.

6. Bake in a 350° oven until the cheese is melted. Garnish with the minced parsley to serve.

Serves 6 to 8

 Brunello di Montalcino

Hearty Vegetable Lasagna

Don't let the length of this recipe scare you off. Your efforts will be well rewarded at the dinner table when you present your guests with this fabulous lasagna. It can be made in advance and freezes well.

Ingredients

Tomato Sauce

4	tablespoons olive oil
1	large yellow onion, diced
3	large shallots, diced
3	large cloves garlic, minced
1	carrot, peeled and finely diced
1	stalk celery, diced
$^1/_2$	bunch parsley, chopped
7	cups canned roma tomatoes, crushed
1	tablespoon *each* dried oregano, thyme and basil
$^1/_2$	teaspoon whole cloves
	Few gratings of nutmeg
$^1/_2$ to $^3/_4$	cup red wine
1	teaspoon undiluted chicken bouillon powder
	Sea salt
	Freshly ground pepper
2	pounds eggplant (or zucchini)

continued on page 77

Method

1. For the tomato sauce, heat the oil in a large pot or saucepan. When oil is hot, add the onions, shallot, garlic, carrot, celery and parsley. Cover and sweat the vegetables for about 10 minutes or until soft.

2. Add the tomatoes, oregano, thyme, basil, cloves, nutmeg, 1/2 cup of the wine and the undiluted bouillon powder. Cover and simmer for at least 40 minutes, using the additional 1/4 cup of wine to thin the sauce, as needed.

3. Taste, adjust the seasonings with salt and pepper and set aside.

4. Meanwhile, slice the eggplant (or zucchini) into 1/4-inch thick slices. Sprinkle both sides generously with salt, place in a colander and let the slices sit for at least 40 minutes to extract all the moisture. Towel dry and set aside.

5. For the pepper-onion mixture, heat 2 tablespoons of oil in a wide frying pan. When the oil is hot, add the red pepper, green pepper, and onion. Sauté together, adding a few twists of pepper while cooking, for about 8 minutes. Remove, transfer to a bowl and set aside.

6. For the mushroom mixture, using the same pan add 1 more tablespoon of oil. When oil is hot, add the mushrooms and sherry. Sauté for about 5 minutes and then add the chopped spinach. Taste and season with salt and pepper. Remove and set aside.

7. Dip the eggplant (or zucchini) into the flour and shake off the excess. Heat the remaining oil in the fry pan. Sauté the eggplant, turning as needed, for about 5 to 8 minutes or until golden brown on both sides. Drain on paper towels.

Ingredients

Pepper-Onion Mixture

5	tablespoons olive oil
1	medium yellow onion, sliced
1	red pepper, seeded and julienned
1	green pepper, seeded and julienned

Mushroom Mixture

$1/2$	pound button mushrooms, sliced
2	tablespoons dry sherry or port
1	large bunch spinach (stems removed), chopped
$1/3$	cup unbleached all-purpose flour
1	pound flat green lasagna noodles

White sauce

4	tablespoons butter
4	tablespoons unbleached flour
2	cups whole milk
	Sea salt
	Freshly ground white pepper
3	cups grated mozzarella cheese
1	cup grated Parmesan cheese
1	bunch fresh basil

Method

8. Meanwhile, cook the noodles in plenty of salted boiling water, as directed, until al dente. Lay them on cloth kitchen towel (not paper towel) until ready to use.

9. For white sauce, melt the butter in a small saucepan. Whisk in the flour and cook, stirring for about 2 minutes. Slowly whisk in the milk, stirring as you go, until the sauce is smooth and thick. Taste and adjust seasonings with salt and pepper. Set aside.

10. To assemble the lasagna, spread about 2/3 of a cup of the tomato sauce on the bottom of 13-inch by 9-inch baking pan. Arrange a layer of cooked noodles on top, then an even layer of eggplant, followed by a thin layer of white sauce. Drizzle some tomato sauce and then add an even layer of mozzarella. Sprinkle with Parmesan and then a layer of basil leaves.

11. Repeat with the next 2 layers, adding the pepper-onion mixture followed by the mushroom mixture. Finish with a layer of noodles, white sauce and finally, cheeses.

12. Preheat oven to 350°. Cover the dish with foil and bake for about 25 minutes. Remove the foil and continue to bake until the cheese is browned and bubbly.

Serves 8 to 10

 Dry White Riesling

*G*nocchi with Classic Italian Sauce

This recipe was given to me by a wonderful Italian neighbour who makes the best gnocchi I have ever eaten. She insists that only red potatoes will do, so I will too. Enjoy.

Ingredients

Sauce

$^1/_2$	cup extra virgin olive oil
1	small yellow onion, finely diced
1	clove garlic, minced
1	pound ground pork
1	pound ground beef
1	16-ounce can roma tomatoes
2	5-ounce cans tomato paste
1	tablespoon chicken bouillon powder, undiluted
$^1/_2$	teaspoon whole cloves
$^1/_4$	teaspoon ground allspice
1	teaspoon sea salt
2	teaspoons freshly ground pepper
$^1/_4$	bunch parsley, finely chopped
$^1/_4$	cup dry red wine
1	piece (about 3 inches) celery
1	piece (about 3 inches) carrot
	Fresh sage

Method

SAUCE

1. Heat the oil in a large frying pan. When hot, add the onion and garlic and sauté over medium heat until lightly brown. Add the beef and pork, breaking it up with a fork, and fry for 10 to 12 minutes or until it becomes browned and somewhat granular in appearance.

2. Transfer the meat to a large pot and add the tomatoes, tomato paste, bouillon, cloves, allspice, salt, pepper, parsley, wine, celery, carrot and sage, stirring to combine. Cover and simmer for about 2 hours. Remove and discard whole cloves.

continued on page 79

Ingredients

Gnocchi

4   large red potatoes

1   cup unbleached all-purpose flour

1   large egg, well beaten

Pinch of freshly grated nutmeg

$^1/_2$ teaspoon sea salt

1   teaspoon freshly ground white pepper

2   tablespoons unsalted butter

    Freshly grated Parmesan cheese

Method

GNOCCHI

3. Meanwhile, peel the potatoes and cook in boiling water for about 25 minutes or until tender. Drain the potatoes and return them to the pot over medium heat for 1 minute to dry them a bit.

4. When cool enough to handle, grate the potatoes into a large bowl. Add the flour, egg , nutmeg, salt and pepper. Mix well to incorporate the ingredients.

5. Turn the potato mixture out onto a floured board and roll the potato mixture into sausage lengths about the diameter of your thumb. Cut into 1-inch pieces and press lightly with the tines of a fork to create a lined pattern on the gnocchi.

6. Bring 3 quarts of salted water to a boil, drop in the gnocchi about 10 at a time, taking care not to overcrowd. Cook just until they rise to the surface. Scoop out with a slotted spoon and place the gnocchi in a buttered serving dish; keep in a warm oven until you are finished.

7. To serve, ladle sauce generously over the gnochhi and top with freshly grated Parmesan cheese.

Serves 8 to 10

 Vermentino di Gallura

Roasted Chicken Lasagna with Wild Mushrooms

I love the flavors of this bistro-style pasta dish. You can use leftover chicken or simply

purchase a spit-roasted whole chicken from your favorite deli.

Ingredients

2   ounces dried wild mushrooms

1   whole roasted chicken (about 2 1/2 pounds)

1   pound spinach lasagna noodles

1/3   cup olive oil

1   large yellow onion, diced

2 or 3   cloves garlic, minced

Sauce

3   tablespoons unsalted butter

1   large shallot, minced

3   heaping tablespoons unbleached flour

2   cups milk

1/2   teaspoon sea salt

2   teaspoons ground white pepper

Few grindings of nutmeg

1/2   cup freshly grated Romano cheese

1/2   cup freshly grated Parmesan cheese

Method

1. Cover the mushrooms with hot water and let them soak for 30 minutes. Drain, squeeze dry, chop and set aside.

2. Meanwhile, remove the chicken meat from the bones. Discard the skin and shred the meat into small bite-size pieces. Set aside.

3. Heat the oil in a fry pan over medium heat. When oil is hot, add the onion and garlic and sauté until the onion is soft. Add the reserved mushrooms and the shredded chicken meat, stirring to combine. Set aside.

4. Meanwhile, melt the butter in a saucepan. Add the shallot and cook over low heat until softened and translucent but not brown. Stir in the flour and cook for about 3 minutes. Whisk in the milk and continue to whisk until the sauce is thick and smooth. Taste and adjust seasonings with salt, pepper and nutmeg. Add the Romano cheese and set aside.

5. Cook the noodles until al dente. When noodles are done, drain and lay them flat on a kitchen towel (not paper toweling) to dry.

6. To assemble, preheat the oven to 350°. Lightly oil the bottom of a shallow 9 by 12-inch baking pan. Spread a portion of the chicken mixture on top, then some of the béchamel sauce and a sprinkling of Parmesan cheese. Top with a layer of the cooked noodles.

7. Repeat 2 more times, finishing with the noodles, sauce and a final sprinkling of cheese. Cover with foil and bake for about 20 minutes.

Serves 8

 Duckhorn Merlot

Creamy Polenta

Polenta is a staple of the Latin kitchen. It can be transformed from a simple side dish into inviting appetizers by grilling it, or a fabulous first course by introducing imported cheeses and condiments into the cooking cornmeal. Either way you choose to prepare the polenta, I'm sure you'll enjoy it.

Ingredients

6 to 7 cups chicken stock

2 cups yellow cornmeal

3/4 cup unsalted butter

3/4 cup freshly grated Parmesan cheese

1 teaspoon sea salt

2 teaspoons freshly ground pepper

Method

1. Bring the chicken stock to a boil. Slowly, in a very thin stream, pour in some of the cornmeal, whisking continuously as you go. It is important that you never stop whisking or the cornmeal will cook in the bottom of the pan and lump together. It will take about 20 minutes of constant whisking to cook the polenta. After about 10 minutes of cooking, stir in the condiments if chosen.

2. If you like a thinner, softer polenta, add the larger quantity of stock. The polenta is cooked when it is smooth to the taste and not granular or gritty.

3. Stir in the butter, Parmesan, salt and pepper and serve immediately.

4. If you want to cut the polenta into shapes, spread the soft polenta on a buttered cookie sheet and chill until set. As soon as it is firm cut into squares, triangles or any shape you prefer. Heat a cast iron pan to high, add a little oil and fry the polenta shapes for about 2 minutes each side, or until golden.

Serves 6 to 8

Grilled Polenta with Summer Ratatouille

Here is a wonderfully seasoned combination of fresh vegetables that are cooked together to give you one of France's classic dishes.

Serve the ratatouille by itself or as I do, over triangles of grilled polenta and topped with grated cheese.

Ingredients

Polenta (use full recipe page 81)

2 medium eggplants, peeled and diced into $^3/_4$-inch cubes

3 medium zucchinis, diced into $^3/_4$-inch cubes

2 tablespoons sea salt

8 to 12 tablespoons extra virgin olive oil

2 large onions, sliced

4 large cloves garlic, minced

2 pounds medium-size roma tomatoes

1 red pepper, seeded and diced

1 green pepper, seeded and diced

1 teaspoon sea salt

2 teaspoons freshly ground pepper

1 teaspoon *each* oregano, thyme, basil and herbes de Provence

2 tablespoons capers

$^3/_4$ cup kalamata olives

$^1/_2$ bunch finely chopped parsley

Grated Parmesan cheese

Method

1. Make polenta as directed on page 81. Press into an oiled 9 by 13-inch glass or stainless steel pan and chill until firm.

2. Meanwhile, place the zucchini and eggplant cubes in a stainless steel or glass pan. Sprinkle generously with salt. Let the vegetables sit for at least 1 hour to degourge or remove the moisture. Drain off the liquid and pat vegetables with paper or kitchen towels until dry.

3. Heat 1/4 cup of the the olive oil in a large sauté pan. Add the eggplant and cook over medium heat for 6 to 8 minutes, or until golden on all sides. Remove eggplant from the pan and set aside. Sauté the zucchini in the same oil for 3 to 5 minutes, then remove and set aside.

4. Add a bit more oil to the pan, as needed, and when hot, add the onions. Sauté for 5 minutes until golden brown and then add the tomatoes, garlic, peppers, salt, pepper and herbs. Simmer, uncovered, for about 30 minutes or until most of the liquid has evaporated. Add the zucchini, eggplant and capers, continue to simmer for an additional 10 minutes. Taste and adjust the seasonings.

5. Meanwhile, trim the chilled polenta into triangles. Brush with olive oil and grill over medium heat, for about 5 minutes per side, or until heated through.

6. Transfer polenta to a serving platter. Spoon ratatouille over the polenta and garnish with the olives and parsley.

Serves 8 to 10

Risotto with Fennel

Risotto is a classic Italian rice dish from the north of Italy. A short-grain rice, Arborio, which has a very high gluten content, gives it the ability to absorb flavors and liquids, thus giving the rice a creaminess while the grain remains firm. The adaptations are endless. Here is one of my versions, but feel free to go for it in your own way.

Ingredients

10	cups chicken stock
4	tablespoons unsalted butter
2	tablespoons virgin olive oil
2	ribs celery, finely diced
1	cup yellow onion, diced
1 to 2	garlic cloves, minced
3	cups Arborio rice
1	cup white wine
1	small fennel bulb, finely julienned
2	tablespoons unsalted butter
$1/3$	cup grated fresh Parmesan cheese
	Sea salt
	Fresh ground white pepper
3	tablespoons chopped fennel tops

Method

1. Heat the stock to a low simmer, keep warm. In a large pot heat the butter and oil, add the celery, onion, garlic and sauté until the mixture is soft but not brown.

2. Add the rice stirring well so that all the grains are well coated, about 3 minutes. Pour in the wine and stir until the wine is absorbed. Stir in the fennel and 1 cup of the warm stock. Stir the rice until the stock is almost absorbed. Add the stock 1 cup at a time, waiting until it is almost absorbed before adding the next, continue in this manner until all but 1 cup of liquid is left to add. The rice should be tender but still firm. This process should take about 20 minutes. Add the remaining butter, Parmesan cheese, salt and pepper to taste. Stir in the remaining stock, continuing to stir until it is absorbed.

3. Place the risotto on a large serving platter and garnish with the chopped fennel tops. Serve immediately.

Serves 6 to 8

 Vernaccia di San Gimignano, Pietrafitta,

Risotto Croquettes

Creamy risotto, made from Italian Arborio rice, is flavored with two types of cheese and then shaped into croquettes before frying. Remember to warm the chicken stock before adding it to the rice.

Ingredients

3	tablespoons olive oil
2	large shallots, finely chopped
1	cup Italian Arborio rice
3	generous cups warm chicken stock
1	large egg, lightly beaten
$1/2$	cup freshly grated Parmesan cheese
2	teaspoons sea salt
1	teaspoon freshly ground pepper
$1/2$	pound Asiago cheese, cut into $1/2$-inch cubes

Method

1. Heat the olive oil in a frying pan. When oil is hot, add the shallots and sauté for about 2 minutes until soft. Stir in the rice and cook for about 1 minute until it becomes translucent, taking care not to let the rice brown.

2. Add the warm stock, a ladleful at a time, stirring well after each addition. Do not add more stock until the liquid in the pot is completely absorbed. Continue this process until the stock is used and the rice is cooked through but not mushy. You must continually stir the rice during cooking.

3. When the rice is cooked, remove from heat and stir in the egg, Parmesan cheese, salt and pepper. Immediately turn the rice onto a baking sheet, spreading it out to cool.

4. When rice is cool enough to handle, form it into balls about the size of golf balls.

5. Push a cube of Asiago cheese into the center. Then lightly flatten the rice ball into a patty. It may be easier to shape the rice by dipping your hands into warm water first. Chill the patties until firm.

6. Heat a nonstick skillet over medium heat. Fry the croquettes for about 8 to 10 minutes, turning once, until light brown and heated through.

7. Transfer to a large serving platter.

Serves 6 to 8

 Trebbiano di Romagna

Wild Rice with Sultana Raisins & Shiitake Mushrooms

This simple but flavorful preparation of wild rice can be served with any of your favorite poultry or fish dishes. If you have leftovers, they make a terrific cold salad served on crisp greens.

Ingredients

1	cup wild rice
3	cups water
3	tablespoons olive oil
2	shallots, minced
3	green onions chopped
1/2	cup sultana raisins
5	fresh shiitake mushrooms, sliced
8	button mushrooms, quartered
	Sea salt
	Freshly ground pepper
1/3	cup pine nuts, toasted

Method

1. Place the rice and water in a pot, cover and bring to the boil. Reduce heat and simmer for about 40 minutes until the rice pops. This means that the kernels actually open up. Monitor the water level while the rice cooks, adding more if necessary. This does not harm the rice's texture or flavor.

2. When the rice is cooked, drain off any excess water and set aside.

3. Heat the oil in a sauté pan. When the oil is hot, add the shallots and onions and sauté for 3 to 5 minutes or just until soft. Add the raisins, shiitakes and button mushrooms and continue to cook for 5 minutes until the mushrooms are soft.

4. Add the cooked rice, stirring evenly to distribute the ingredients. Taste and adjust the seasonings with salt and pepper.

5. To serve, spoon the rice onto a serving platter and garnish with the toasted pine nuts.

Serves 6

Entrees

French Roasted Free-range Chicken

Blue Cornmeal Chicken with Tomatillo Salsa

Ginger Sesame Chicken Burgers

Chicken Provencal with Wild Mushrooms

Baked Portuguese-style Chicken

Turkey & Turtle Bean Chili

Turkey Tonnato

Grilled Quail with Sun-dried Cherries

Duck Breast with Green Peppercorn & Mustard Sauce

Veal Scallops with Demi-glace

Osso Buco

Veal Chops with Roasted Chestnuts & Caramelized Onions

Southern Style Beef

Caren's Pepper Steak with Oven Fries

Rolled Italian Beef Roast with Artichokes

Indian Lamb Curry

Leg of Lamb with Shiitake Mushrooms & Roasted Garlic

Lamb Chop

Pork & Cashew Stir-fry

Grilled Fish with Herbed Tomato Relish

Pacific Coast Halibut Cheeks

Tuna Fillet with Tapenade

Fresh Sea Bass with Shallots, Chives & Cream

Poached Salmon with Spinach & Vermouth Sauce

Marinated Salmon Fillet with Ginger

Cataplana

Grilled Asian Scallops

Black Bean Prawns

José's Cracked Crab

Prawns & Caperberries

Shuckers Fried Squid

French Roasted Free-range Chicken

If you have never eaten a free-range or free-run chicken before, now is the time. Essentially they are hormone and chemical free.

These chickens have the flavor that was common years ago. The cost is a little higher, but in my opinion,

the added price buys more than double the taste.

Ingredients

1	3 to 4 pound free-range chicken
2	tablespoons olive oil
1	tablespoon sweet Hungarian paprika
1	tablespoon chopped fresh thyme
1	tablespoon chopped fresh rosemary
1/2	teaspoon freshly ground pepper
1/4	teaspoon sea salt
1	pound russet potatoes, peeled and quartered
1	head garlic, peeled and left whole
1/2	cup white wine
1/2	cup chicken stock

Method

1. Wash and dry the chicken, place the neck, gizzard & heart inside the cavity, set aside. In a small bowl, mix the oil, paprika, thyme, rosemary, pepper & salt. Rub this mixture all over the chicken. Truss or tie the legs together. Place the chicken in a roasting pan, set aside.

2. Preheat the oven to 375°. Scatter the potatoes and garlic cloves around the chicken. Cover the roaster, place in the oven and bake. Turn the potatoes at 30-minute intervals so that they brown evenly. Bake for 1 1/2 to 2 hours or until the juices run clear. The internal temperature of the chicken should be 170°. Never serve chicken undercooked. After 1 hour of roasting, remove the lid and finish by cooking uncovered to brown.

3. Remove the chicken from the pan to a serving platter and let it rest for about 10 minutes before carving. Remove the potatoes and garlic and keep warm. Meanwhile, place the empty roasting pan on low heat, add the wine and chicken stock to the pan and bring to a boil, making sure that you scrape the brown bits from the bottom of the pan. Adjust the seasoning with sea salt and freshly ground pepper.

4. Pour the pan juices over the sliced chicken, potatoes and garlic. Serve immediately.

Serves 4 to 5

 Jean Durup, Chablis Premier Cru

Blue Cornmeal Chicken with Tomatillo Salsa

Tomatillos, dry-roasted in a pan along with roma tomatoes, whole garlic and a jalapeño pepper,

are chopped and then mixed with a little tequila to make a marvelous, full-flavored salsa.

Ingredients

Salsa

4 or 5   medium tomatillos, husked

4 or 5   roma tomatoes

$^1/_2$ large white onion, quartered

6   whole unpeeled garlic cloves

$^1/_2$ small jalapeño peppers, seeded and diced

$^1/_3$ cup tequila

  Sea salt

  Freshly ground pepper

Filling

$^1/_2$ pound chèvre

2   cloves garlic, minced

$^1/_2$ cup chopped cilantro

1   teaspoon ground cumin

1   tablespoon freshly ground pepper

1   small whole jalapeño pepper

6   boneless skinless chicken breasts

1   whole egg, lightly beaten

1   cup blue cornmeal

3   tablespoons olive oil for frying

Method

1. To make salsa, preheat oven to 400°. Place the tomatillos, tomatoes, onion, whole garlic and whole jalapeño in a heavy cast iron skillet. Do not add any oil. Place the pan over high heat and roast the vegetables quickly, shaking the pan around to help brown them on all sides.

2. Transfer to the oven and roast for 15 to 20 minutes or until the tomatoes are blistered and very dark in color. Remember to shake the pan occasionally.

3. Remove from the oven and set aside. When the garlic is cool enough to handle, remove the papery skin. Remove and discard the stem from the jalapeño.

4. Transfer all the ingredients to a food processor fitted with a metal blade. Pulse about 10 times, then add the tequila, salt and pepper. Pulse a few more times, just until the it begins to break down. You want the salsa to remain a little chunky rather than a complete purée. Set aside.

5. Meanwhile, combine the chèvre, garlic, cilantro, cumin, minced jalapeño and pepper, stirring until blended. Set aside.

6. Cut the chicken breast in half and remove the bony gristle; reserve the small filet piece for another use.

7. Cut a pocket in the thickest end of the breast. Spoon a generous tablespoon of the cheese mixture into the pocket and press to seal edges. Dip each breast into the beaten egg and then generously dust with cornmeal on all sides. Press in gently to coat both sides well.

8. Heat a cast iron skillet to medium. When hot, add 1 to 2 tablespoons olive oil. Arrange the chicken in the pan and cook for about 15 minutes, turning once, until the chicken in brown on both sides. It should not be pink inside.

9. To serve, slice the chicken on the diagonal. Flare the pieces out on the plate and garnish with a spoonful of salsa.

Serves 4 to 6

 Blanc de Blancs

Ginger Sesame Chicken Burgers

Finely minced chicken, green onion, fresh ginger, hoisin sauce and other Asian ingredients are combined in these not-so-typical burgers. You can fry them in a small amount of peanut oil or grill them on the barbecue.

Ingredients

1	pound boneless, skinless chicken meat
3	green onions, finely sliced
1	tablespoon minced fresh ginger
1	medium clove garlic, minced
1	tablespoon sesame oil
1	tablespoon hoisin sauce
1	tablespoon fish sauce
1	teaspoon minced fermented black beans
1	teaspoon chili flakes
1/2	teaspoon sea salt
1/2	cup black sesame seeds
	Peanut oil or vegetable oil, for frying

Method

1. Mince the chicken in a food processor fitted with a metal blade, taking care not to overprocess. A meat grinder also works well.

2. Transfer the chicken to a bowl and add the green onions, ginger, garlic, sesame oil, hoisin sauce, fish sauce, black beans, chili flakes and salt. Mix well to incorporate all of the seasonings.

3. Shape the chicken mixture into six patties and then dip both sides of each patty into the sesame seeds.

4. Heat a small amount of peanut oil in a nonstick skillet. When the oil is hot, fry the burgers for about 5 minutes per side, turning once, or until the burgers are cooked through. (For grilling, cook the burgers over medium coals for 4 to 5 minutes per side, turning once, or until cooked through.)

5. Serve on a bun garnished with arugula or on a bed of steamed Chinese greens.

Serves 6

 Sapporo beer

Chicken Provencal with Wild Mushrooms

Inspiration for this dish comes from a small village in Provence called Vaison la Romaine. We tasted this fabulous chicken on one of our culinary tours to France, while dining under café umbrellas along the main street in Vaison.

Ingredients

$1/4$ cup *each* dried morels, boletus and cèpes (or other wild mushrooms)

$1/4$ cup all-purpose flour

5   tablespoons olive oil

2   pounds chicken thighs, skin removed

1   large yellow onion, finely diced

8   large whole cloves garlic, peeled

2   tablespoons chicken bouillon powder, undiluted

1   bay leaf

   Freshly ground pepper

$1 1/2$ cups fresh button mushrooms, sliced

1   cup dry white wine

$1/2$ cup heavy cream

$1/4$ bunch fresh parsley, finely chopped

Method

1. Soak the dried wild mushrooms in 2 cups of warm water for about 40 minutes or until reconstituted. Squeeze them every 15 minutes or so to help absorb the water.

2. Meanwhile, heat 3 tablespoons of the olive oil in a cast iron pan and place the flour in a shallow dish.

3. Dip the chicken into the flour, shaking off the excess, and arrange in the frying pan. Cook, turning the pieces as needed, for about 10 minutes or until the chicken is golden brown on both sides. Transfer to a roasting pan and set aside.

4. Wipe out any excess oil and flour sediment from the frying pan, then heat the remaining 2 tablespoons of oil. When hot, add the onion and garlic. Lightly sauté for about 5 minutes or until the onion begins to soften.

5. Drain the mushrooms and if they seem a little sandy, rinse them again in water. Chop the larger mushrooms, if desired, and add to the pan of sautéed onions along with the bouillon powder, bay leaf, pepper, fresh mushrooms and wine. Cook for a few minutes, until the boullion dissolves, and then pour over the chicken.

6. Cover the pan and bake at 350° for 1 1/2 hours, or until the chicken is cooked through. Remove, transfer to a serving platter, cover and keep warm.

7. Remove the garlic cloves, put them in a small bowl and mash with the back of a spoon. Return garlic to the roaster, add the cream, and bring sauce to a boil. Taste and adjust the seasonings. Spoon sauce over the chicken and garnish with chopped parsley.

Serves 4 to 6

 Côtes du Luberon, red wine

Baked Portuguese-style Chicken

My husband José, who comes from Setubal, Portugal, loves Mediterranean flavors so I created this

hearty chicken recipe using his favorite ingredients—spicy chorizo, anchovies and Moroccan dried oil-cured olives.

Ingredients

16 chicken thighs

¹/₂ cup all-purpose flour

8 tablespoons olive oil

1 large onion, diced

6 to 8 cloves garlic, minced

1 2-ounce can anchovies, chopped

4 cups canned Italian plum tomatoes, drained

1 cup reserved canned tomato liquid

1 bay leaf

2 tablespoons balsamic vinegar

1 cup sun-dried tomatoes

1 cup dried oil-cured olives

1 14-ounce can water-packed artichoke hearts, drained and cut into eighths

1 pound Portuguese chorizo, sliced

¹/₂ bunch fresh parsley finely chopped

Method

1. Remove the skin from the chicken and lightly coat both sides in the flour. Heat half of the oil in a heavy skillet. When oil is hot, add the chicken and cook for 10 to 15 minutes or until golden brown on all sides. Transfer to a roasting pan and set aside.

2. If the bottom of the skillet is stuck with a lot of flour, wipe it out. If not, add the remaining half of the oil. When oil is hot, add the onion, garlic and anchovy. Sauté for about 8 minutes until the onion is soft and the anchovy is dissolved.

3. Using kitchen scissors, cut the tomatoes directly into the pan. This way the juice doesn't get all over the counter. Add the bay leaf and vinegar, stirring to combine. Cook for about 5 minutes or until the tomatoes begin to soften and break up.

4. Spoon the tomato mixture over the chicken. Cover and bake in a 350° oven for 40 minutes. Turn over chicken and add the sun-dried tomatoes, olives and artichoke hearts to the pan. Cover and return to the oven for an additional 45 minutes, or until the chicken is tender and cooked through.

5. Meanwhile, cut the chorizo into 1/4-inch thick slices and fry over medium heat until crisp.

6. To serve, turn the chicken out onto a colorful serving platter and garnish with the chorizo and a sprinkling of parsley.

Serves 6 to 8

 Douro Red Reserve

Turkey Turtle Bean Chili

A break from the traditional beef-and-kidney-bean chili. I have combined southwest spices with black beans and turkey to give you a chili packed with flavor and less fat.

Ingredients

2	cups black turtle beans, cooked
1/2	cup olive oil
2	medium red onions, diced
4	garlic cloves, minced
1	large leek, white part only, diced
1	cup diced celery
1	cup fresh mild Anaheim chilies, chopped
1/4	cup unbleached all-purpose flour
4	cups chicken stock
1	tablespoon Mexican oregano
3	tablespoons hot chili powder
3 to 4	tablespoons cumin
1	teaspoon sea salt
1	cup red bell pepper, diced
2	cups kernel corn
4	cups cooked turkey meat, shredded
1	cup chopped cilantro
2	tablespoons crushed chili flakes

Method

1. Cover the beans with plenty of cold water and drain as soon as they come to a boil. Cover with fresh water, bring to a boil once again, drain. Cover the beans for a third time with fresh water and bring to a boil. Once they boil, turn them down to simmer and continue cook until they are cooked through, about 40 to 60 minutes.

2. In a large saucepan, add the oil, onion, garlic, peppers, leeks, celery and chilies. Sauté for 10 minutes, covered. Stir in the flour and cook an additional 3 minutes. Whisk in the stock, add the oregano, chili powder, cumin, salt, red bell pepper, corn and beans. Stir well to combine all the ingredients. Let the chili simmer for 15 minutes.

3. Add the shredded turkey, cilantro and chili flakes. Simmer for an additional 10 minutes. Serve with warm cornbread.

Serves 6 to 8

 Corona Extra beer

Turkey Tonnato

Tuna gives this Piedmontese sauce its name and its flavor. It is traditionally served over cold veal, however I choose to use roasted turkey breast when veal is expensive or hard to come by. Your can also serve it over steamed chilled asparagus or anywhere a rich sauce is desired.

Ingredients

Turkey

2 $\frac{1}{2}$ to 3 pounds fresh turkey breast

1 to 2 tablespoons olive oil

Freshly ground pepper

$\frac{1}{4}$ teaspoon sea salt

Foil for wrapping the turkey

Tonnato Sauce

1   6-ounce can good quality tuna

2   egg yolks

4   garlic cloves, chopped

4   anchovy fillets, more if desired

$\frac{1}{4}$ cup fresh lemon juice

1   cup extra virgin olive oil

Sea salt

Freshly ground pepper to taste

Minced fresh parsley for garnish

Method

TURKEY

1. Preheat the oven to 350°. Rub the turkey breast with the olive oil, salt and pepper. Place in a baking tray and cover loosely with the foil. Bake for about 50 to 60 minutes, or until the turkey is cooked through. It should not be pink. Set aside to cool.

TONNATO SAUCE

2. In the bowl of a food processor or blender, place the tuna, yolks, garlic, anchovy and lemon juice. Process until the mixture becomes a very smooth paste. Very slowly, with the machine running, pour the oil in. As the blade turns it will emulsify the dressing and create a velvety sauce.

3. Adjust the taste with freshly ground pepper and salt. I don't think you will need much salt as the anchovies provide a lot.

4. Slice the turkey into about 1/8-inch slices, lay them on a long tray slightly overlapping, pour the sauce in a thin line down the center of the turkey. Place the remaining sauce on the side.

5. Garnish the tray with minced parsley.

Serves 6

 Orvieto Classico

Grilled Quail with Sun-dried Cherries

The sun-dried cherry sauce is the perfect mate for these delectable little birds. The sauce of course can be made ahead, making this an excellent dinner party dish. For non-quail-lovers, try chicken or duck as a substitute.

Ingredients

6	boneless quails
1/2	cup olive oil
1	clove garlic, minced
	Sea salt
	Freshly ground pepper
3	tablespoons olive oil
3	shallots, minced
4	whole cloves garlic, peeled
1	cup beef stock
1/3	cup minced parsley
1/4	cup balsamic vinegar
1	cup sun-dried cherries
	Sprigs of fresh sage

Method

1. Combine 1/2 cup of the oil, the minced garlic, and 1/2 teaspoon each of salt and pepper, mixing it into an oily paste.

2. Lay the quail flat in a shallow glass pan and pour the marinade over top, turning to coat both sides. Cover and set aside.

3. Meanwhile, heat the 3 tablespoons of oil in a sauté pan. When oil is hot, add the shallots and sauté for about 2 minutes or until softened. Add the whole garlic and cook for an additional 2 minutes.

4. Pour in the stock and add the parsley, sage, vinegar, cherries and 1 large sprig of sage. Reduce heat and simmer for about 20 minutes or until the sauce begins to thicken slightly. Taste and adjust seasonings with the salt and pepper.

5. Remove and discard the sage. Remove the whole garlic and mash it to a pulp with a fork. Return it to the sauce, stirring to combine.

6. Heat a grill or barbecue to medium. Lift quail from marinade and arrange flat on the grill. Cook for about 3 minutes and turn over. Continue to grill, basting with marinade as needed, for 3 to 5 minutes longer or until cooked.

7. Transfer quail to a serving platter and ladle half of the sauce over the birds, reserving the rest to pass at the table. Garnish with the additional sprigs of fresh sage.

Serves 6

Henri Bourgeois Sancerre Blanc

Duck Breast with Green Peppercorn & Mustard Sauce

Here on the west coast we have some terrific duck farms growing lean and tasty birds, so don't believe the old myths about duck being

fatty. In fact, I think it is a great alternative to chicken or turkey—particularly in dark-meat dishes. Try duck. You'll love it.

Ingredients

2 to 3 tablespoons olive oil

3 whole duck breasts

Sea salt

Freshly ground pepper

Sauce

2 tablespoons unsalted butter

2 tablespoons unbleached all-purpose flour

1 1/2 cups chicken stock

2 tablespoons grainy Dijon mustard

2 tablespoons brined green peppercorns, drained

3 tablespoons heavy cream

Sea salt

Freshly ground pepper

1/2 cup brandy

Method

1. Melt the butter in a medium saucepan, add the flour and cook for about 2 minutes. Whisk in the chicken stock and continue to whisk until the sauce becomes smooth and thick. Stir in the mustard, peppercorns and heavy cream. Adjust the seasoning with salt and pepper. Set the sauce aside.

2. Cut the duck breasts in half. Season both sides with salt and pepper. Heat a cast iron pan to medium. Sear the duck breasts on both sides to seal in the juices. Continue to fry the breast for about 15 minutes or until an instant-read thermometer reaches 140° internal temperature.

3. Remove the duck breast from the pan; let it rest for 1 to 2 minutes. Pour the brandy into the pan and deglaze. Pour this pan juice into the peppercorn sauce and stir well.

4. Slice the duck breasts on the diagonal and serve with the peppercorn sauce. The wild rice on page 85 would be a great side dish.

Serves 6

 Merlot or Pinot Noir

Veal Scallops with Demi-glace

The flavour of veal takes on a new dimension with the addition of procuitto and Asiago.

The demi-glace can be used anytime you need a rich brown sauce.

Ingredients

Demi-glace

2   tablespoons butter

1   carrot, chopped

1   chopped onion

3   sprigs fresh parsley

     Pinch of thyme

1   small bay leaf

2   tablespoons flour

2   cups beef stock

1   tablespoon tomato paste

     Salt and freshly ground pepper

$^1/_4$ cup brandy

$^1/_4$ cup Madeira

Veal

6   scallops of veal

$^1/_3$ cup flour, for dredging

3 to 4 tablespoons olive oil

2   garlic cloves, minced

3   ounces of prosciutto, sliced thin

3   ounces of Asiago cheese

Method

DEMI-GLACE

1. Melt the butter in a heavy-bottomed pot. Add the carrot, onion, parsley, thyme & bay leaf. Brown thoroughly, stir and scrape the brown bits from the bottom of the pan. The mixture will look as if it is burnt; it is not. The darker the color of the vegetables, the richer the taste. Keep on medium heat, with the lid on for 15 minutes.

2. Add the flour and cook 5 more minutes. Whisk in the stock and continue to simmer for 30 more minutes. Strain the sauce through a fine metal sieve pressing hard to ensure all the sauce is pressed out. Add the tomato paste, salt and pepper to taste. Just before you are ready to serve, add the brandy and Madeira, heat through.

VEAL

3. Dredge the veal in the flour and shake off the excess. Set aside.

4. Heat the oil in a fry pan, add the garlic, then quickly fry the veal in a hot pan, searing each side for no more than a minute.

5. Lay a slice of the prosciutto on top of the veal, then top with the Asiago cheese. Place in a warm oven just to melt the cheese.

6. Place the veal on the plate, generously pour the warmed demi-glace sauce over.

Serves 6

 Duckhorn Cabernet Sauvignon

Osso Buco

Meaty veal shanks, slow-cooked in this flavorful, classic recipe, may be accompanied by a risotto, creamy polenta or old-fashioned mashed potatoes.

Ingredients

6   veal shanks, cut from the hind shank

5   tablespoons olive oil

4   tablespoons butter

$^1/_2$ cup unbleached all-purpose flour

2   large onions, diced

2   medium carrots, peeled and
     finely diced

1   celery stalk, finely diced

3   large cloves garlic, minced

$^1/_2$ bunch parsley, chopped

2   cups canned roma tomatoes, chopped

2   sprigs fresh sage

2   bay leaves

1   cup beef stock

1   cup dry white wine

     Sea salt

     Freshly ground pepper

Method

1. Heat 2 tablespoons each of oil and butter in a heavy cast iron pan. Dip the veal shanks into the flour, shaking off the excess, and sear them in the hot pan for 4 to 6 minutes until golden brown on both sides. Remove and set aside.

2. In the same pan, heat the remaining 3 tablespoons oil and 2 tablespoons butter. When hot, add the onion, carrots, celery, garlic and parsley. Sauté for 10 minutes until soft.

3. Add the tomatoes, sage, bay leaves, stock, wine, salt and pepper. Cook over medium heat for about 15 minutes so that the flavors marry.

4. Preheat the oven to 350°. Spoon a small portion of the vegetable mixture on the bottom of the baking pan. Arrange the veal shanks on top in a single layer. Top with the remaining vegetables.

5. Cover the pan with foil and bake for 2 1/2 to 3 hours. Check the pan from time to time to ensure that it doesn't dry out. Add a little more wine if required.

6. To serve, transfer the shanks and the pan juices to a serving platter and sprinkle with chopped parsley.

Serves 6

  Barbaresco

Veal Chops with Roasted Chestnuts and Caramelized Onions

This basic veal chop is made special with the roasting of chestnuts and caramelization of onions. The condiment is so delicious,

don't save it for veal alone. I use it to accent and garnish my Christmas turkey. There is never a crumb left.

Ingredients

Chestnut Mixture

1	pound Italian chestnuts
1/2	pound silverskin onions or small shallots
3	tablespoons unsalted butter
2	teaspoons sugar

1/2 to 1/3 cup white wine

Sea salt and cracked pepper to taste

Meat

2 to 3 tablespoons olive oil

3	garlic cloves, chopped
6	thick veal chops, about 8 to 10 ounces each
1/4	cup unbleached all-purpose flour, for dredging
1/2	teaspoon sea salt
1	teaspoon freshly ground pepper

Method

1. Preheat the oven to 350°. With a sharp knife, make a cross on the flat side of the chestnuts. Place all the chestnuts on a cookie sheet and bake them for about 1 hour. Shake the pan occasionally during baking.

2. Meanwhile, bring a large pot of water to the boil, drop the onions in the water and let them blanch for about 5 minutes. Remove and place in cold water at once to make the peeling much easier. Peel when cool enough to handle.

3. Remove the chestnuts from the oven and peel right away. If you wait until the chestnuts are cool the inside skin will adhere to the nut and make peeling impossible. Use gloves if necessary.

4. Meanwhile, in fry pan, prepare the veal. Heat the olive oil to medium, add the chopped garlic and sauté until the garlic begins to turn dark brown.

5. Mix together the flour, salt and pepper. Dredge the chops in the flour mixture, lightly coating each side.

6. In the cast iron pan, sprinkle sugar on the onions and shake the pan to promote caramelization or browning. Cut the chestnuts into quarters and toss them into the pan. Let them heat through about 5 minutes. Pour in the wine and let it reduce to almost nothing, season with the salt and pepper. Serve over the chop.

7. While the onion/chestnut mixture is reducing, cook the veal in the garlic/oil. Remove the garlic and fry the chops on medium-high heat for 3 to 4 minutes each side for medium, less for rare meat.

Serves 6

 Stags' Leap Petite Syrah

Southern Style Beef

This is more glamorous than stews with potatoes and peas, and the flavors are much more fun.

It's even better the next day, if there's any left. Serve it with warmed tortillas or fresh bread.

Ingredients

3	tablespoons olive oil
1	large yellow onion, diced
1	bunch green onions, sliced thin
3	garlic cloves, minced
2	yellow peppers, cut into medium dice
2	green peppers, cut into medium dice
4	large roma tomatoes, cored and diced
2	fresh Anaheim peppers, diced, *or*
1	14-ounce can Anaheim peppers, drained and diced
1	teaspoon ground cumin
2	tablespoons pure chili powder
2	teaspoons dry oregano
1	bunch fresh cilantro, chopped
8	cups beef stock
	Sea salt
	Freshly ground pepper
1/4	cup unsalted butter
1/4	cup unbleached flour
1/4	cup olive oil
2	pounds top sirloin, trimmed of fat and cut into 1 inch dice
1 to 4	fresh jalapeños, sliced
1/2	cup grated jack cheese
1/2	cup grated cheddar cheese
1/2	cup red pepper, finely diced
1/2	cup chopped cilantro

Method

1. Heat the olive oil in a large pot, add the onion, green onions, garlic, yellow pepper and green pepper. Sauté covered for about 5 minutes, stirring occasionally.

2. Add the tomatoes, Anaheim peppers, cumin, chili powder, oregano, cilantro and stock. Let the mixture simmer for 30 minutes.

3. In a small sauté pan, heat the butter until lightly browned, stir in the flour and cook for about 2 minutes. Take about 1 cup of liquid from the simmering sauce and whisk it into the flour until it is smooth. Pour this back into the sauce and stir until it begins to thicken. Season with salt and pepper.

4. In a cast iron pan heat the olive oil. When the pan is hot, add the beef and brown well on all sides, toss in the sliced jalapeños to suit your taste. Season with salt and pepper. As soon as the beef is browned, transfer it to the simmering sauce. Let it cook for 10 minutes to marry the flavor. Adjust the seasonings to taste.

5. To serve, ladle into bowls, generously garnish with the cheeses, red pepper and cilantro.

Serves 6

 Chilean Merlot

Caren's Pepper Steak with Oven Fries

"Meat and potatoes" takes on a new meaning with this bistro-style entrée.

You can purchase five-blend peppercorns whole, as described in the recipe, or already ground.

Ingredients

Oven Fries

6 to 8 russet potatoes

Sea salt

Freshly ground pepper

$^1/_3$ cup olive oil

Meat

6 New York strip loins (about 8 ounces *each*)

$^1/_2$ cup five-blend peppercorns

2 tablespoons butter

2 tablespoons olive oil

$^1/_3$ cup brandy

2 or 3 shallots, minced

1 clove garlic, minced

2 tablespoons Dijon mustard

$^3/_4$ cup rich beef stock

$^3/_4$ cup heavy cream

Sea salt

Method

1. For the fries, preheat oven to 450°. Peel the potatoes if you don't like the skin. Cut them into French fries but not too thin.

2. Bring a large pot of salted water to a boil, blanch the potatoes in the water and let them boil for about 5 minutes.

3. Drain immediately, taking care not to let them overcook. Place potatoes in a single layer on a cookie sheet. Drizzle with olive oil, salt and pepper.

4. Bake for about 40 minutes or until the potatoes are golden brown, turning them occasionally during baking.

5. Meanwhile, trim any excess fat from the steaks. Place the peppercorns in a plastic bag and crush them with a rolling pin (or grind them in a mini chopper). Press the crushed peppercorns into the steaks, a little or a lot depending on how spicy you like it.

6. Heat a cast iron pan over medium heat. Add the butter and the oil. When hot, add the steaks and cook for 3 to 4 minutes per side, turning once, for medium. Remove the steaks from the pan and keep warm. Add the brandy to the pan and ignite, taking care to keep the flame away from the exhaust system.

7. Stir in the shallots and garlic and sauté briefly until they become translucent. Pour in the beef stock, increase the heat to high and reduce the liquid by half.

8. Whisk in the mustard and heavy cream. Then reduce heat and simmer for 10 to 15 minutes or until sauce thickens. Taste and adjust seasonings.

9. To serve, arrange steaks on a serving platter and spoon some of the sauce over the top. Surround the edges of the platter with oven fries and offer remaining sauce at the table.

Serves 6

 Duckhorn, Napa Valley, Howell Mountain
Cabernet Sauvignon

Rolled Italian Beef Roast with Artichokes

Spicy capicollo and cool-tasting asparagus are tucked inside this roasted roll of beef. Ask your butcher to cut the inside round about 1 inch thick and to butterfly it. Another tip, to make peeling onions easy, I quickly blanch them in boiling water first and then skin just slides off.

Ingredients

1   inside beef round (about 2 pounds), cut 1 inch thick

3 or 4 cloves garlic, minced

1   teaspoon coarsely cracked pepper

4   ounces capicollo, thinly sliced

8   spears fresh asparagus, trimmed (or canned)

6   ounces Asiago cheese, grated

Kitchen string

Olive oil, for rubbing

Garniture

1   14-ounce can water-packed artichokes, drained and cut into eighths

1/2 pound silverskin onions, peeled

Method

1. Preheat the oven to 375°. Open up and lay the beef on a flat surface and using a meat pounder, gently pound it to an even thickness. Rub the garlic over the surface and sprinkle with the pepper.

2. Arrange the capicollo slices evenly over 3/4 of the meat. Arrange the asparagus, in a lengthwise strip, down the center of the beef. Sprinkle the entire surface with the grated cheese.

3. Roll the beef up lengthwise and tie with kitchen string at intervals that are spaced about 2 inches apart.

4. Lightly rub the beef roll with olive oil. Place in a hot cast iron skillet (or other ovenproof pan) and sauté over medium heat for 5 to 8 minutes or until browned on all sides.

5. Remove pan from heat. Scatter artichokes and onions around the beef. Transfer the pan to the oven and roast for 20 to 25 minutes, turning the meat at 10-minute intervals.

6. To serve, remove kitchen string and slice. Serve with pan juices.

Serves 6

Barbera

Indian Lamb Curry

Curry is a taste that you either love or hate. Sometimes you're able to warm up to it if the spices are subtle.

This Indian curry is sweeter and thicker that the Thai-style curries, which tend to be very thin and fiery hot. The lamb

complements this sauce well, however beef or pork would be a suitable alternative.

Ingredients

2 pounds boneless lamb strip loins

 Flour for dredging

3 to 4 tablespoons peanut oil

3 garlic cloves, minced

1 medium onion, diced

1 teaspoon freshly ground pepper

Sauce

3 tablespoons unsalted butter

1 large yellow onion, diced

2 garlic cloves, minced

1 small congo or serrano pepper,
 finely diced

3 tablespoons curry powder

2 cups coconut milk

1 cup whole milk

1 tablespoon undiluted chicken
 bouillon powder

4 tablespoons chutney

 Juice of 1/2 lemon

 Sea salt

 Freshly ground pepper

Method

1. Cut any membrane or fat from the lamb. Cut into 1-inch cubes. Dredge in the flour and set aside.

2. Heat a cast iron pan to medium-high, add the oil, garlic, onion and floured lamb. Sear the lamb very quickly on all sides, about 5 minutes, not longer. Remove from the pan and set aside.

3. In the same pan melt the butter, add the diced large onion, garlic and hot pepper. Sauté for about 5 minutes or until soft. Stir in the curry powder and cook for 1 more minute. Whisk in both the milks, being very careful not to let the mixture boil. Keep it on simmer. Add the undiluted stock, chutney and lemon juice. Let the sauce simmer for about 30 minutes, adjust the seasoning with salt and pepper.

4. To serve, heat the sauce, add the reserved lamb to the sauce, being careful not to overcook the lamb. Accompany the curry with rice and assorted condiments.

Condiments: coconut, raisins, bananas, cashews, chutney, hot pepper.

Serves 6

 Kingfisher Indian Lager

Leg of Lamb with Shiitake Mushrooms & Roasted Garlic

This leg of lamb is smothered in a grainy Dijon, garlic, and rosemary crust. This bakes onto the lamb, keeping the meat moist inside. With the pan juices, shiitake mushrooms and roasted garlic, lamb takes on a brand new taste dimension.

Ingredients

2   whole heads fresh garlic

1   tablepoon olive oil

1   boneless leg of lamb (about 5 pounds)

5   whole garlic cloves, peeled and sliced lengthwise

Paste

$^1/_2$ cup olive oil

$^1/_2$ cup coarse-textured mustard

3   tablespoons chopped fresh rosemary

2   teaspoons herbes de Provence

1   tablespoons coarsely ground pepper

1   clove garlic, minced

5 or 6 fresh shiitake mushrooms

1   cup dry red wine

1   cup beef stock

Sea salt

Freshly ground pepper

Method

1. Preheat oven to 325°. To roast the garlic, cut 1/4 inch off the top of each head. Rub all over with olive oil and place in a garlic roaster, or wrap loosely in foil. Bake for 45 to 60 minutes, depending on the size of the garlic, or until the cloves are golden brown and begin to pop from the head. When they are cool enough to handle squeeze out and set aside.

2. Meanwhile, trim any excess fat from the lamb. Using a small knife, make a number of evenly spaced 1-inch slits into the flesh of the lamb. Insert a piece of raw garlic into each slit.

3. Preheat the oven to 450°.

4. Combine the oil, mustard, rosemary, herbes de Provence, pepper and the minced garlic, mixing it into make a paste. Rub the entire leg with the paste and place in a roasting pan. Sear the meat for 10 to 15 minutes in the hot oven, then reduce the temperature to 350°.

5. Continue to roast, calculating 10 minutes per pound (including searing time) for rare, 12 to 15 minutes per pound for medium and 20 minutes per pound for well done.

6. When the lamb is done, transfer to a carving board and keep warm.

7. Remove any excess grease from the roasting pan and place over medium heat. Add the stock and wine to deglaze the pan. Cook over medium heat until the liquid is reduced by half. Add the shiitakes and cook for about 3 more minutes.

8. Return the reserved roasted garlic to the pan, taste and adjust seasonings with salt and pepper.

9. Slice the lamb and spoon mushroom demi-glace over to serve.

Serves 6 to 8

 Stags' Leap Winery Petite Syrah

Herb Crusted Lamb Chops

When you purchase the meat, ask the butcher for double loin chops. They are much meatier than the basic rib chops.

We have wonderful Salt Spring Island lamb here on the coast, and as cottage farming becomes more prominent, people in other

areas are able to obtain superb quality meats more easily.

Ingredients

6   double loin lamb chops about

      6 ounces each, 1 1/2 inches thick

2   tablespoons fresh thyme, chopped

2   tablespoons fresh rosemary, chopped

2   tablespoons fresh basil, chopped

1   tablespoon fresh savory, chopped

1   tablespoon fresh sage, chopped

1   teaspoon sea salt

2   teaspoons freshly ground pepper

3   tablespoons olive oil

Method

1. Trim the lamb of any visible fat. Set aside.

2. Mix together the thyme, rosemary, basil, savory, sage, salt and pepper. Press the herb mixture onto both sides of the lamb chops.

3. Heat a grill or cast iron pan to high, add the oil to the pan, or brush the grill with some oil. Cook the lamb for about 4 minutes each side, (for medium rare) turning only once. Remove from the pan.

4. Serve the lamb immediately. The risotto with fennel on page 83 would be a perfect side dish.

Serves 6

 Châteauneuf-du-Pape

Caren's Pepper Steak with Oven Fries (page 100)

Portuguese Cataplana (page 116)

Poached Salmon with Spinach-Vermouth Sauce (page 114)

Blue Cornmeal Chicken with Tomatillo Salsa (page 88)

Pork and Cashew Stir-fry

Stir-fry meals are quick, fresh and nutritious. Served with steamed rice it is one of my favorite meals.

I am usually on the run, so stir-fries suit a lifestyle that likes to eat well and in a hurry.

Ingredients

Marinade

1	tablespoon soy sauce
1	tablespoon sesame oil
1/4	cup sweet wine or sherry
2	tablespoons cornstarch

2	pounds pork tenderloin
8 to 10	Chinese mushrooms
3 or 4	tablespoons peanut oil
1	large onion, cut into large dice
3	cloves garlic, minced
2	tablespoons minced ginger
1/3	cup hoisin sauce
2	tablespoons rice wine vinegar
2 to 3	tablespoons soy sauce
1/2	pound white button mushrooms
1/3	cup beef stock
1/2	pound snow peas, trimmed
1/2	cup chopped cilantro
	Scotch bonnet peppers
1	cup cashews, toasted
	Steamed rice

Method

1. Soak the mushrooms in enough water to cover for about 30 minutes or until soft. Drain, squeeze out any excess liquid and cut into julienne.

2. Meanwhile, trim any fat off the pork and cut into medium-size cubes.

3. For the marinade, combine the soy, sesame oil, wine and cornstarch. Add the pork and set aside to marinate briefly.

4. Heat 1 or 2 tablespoons oil in a wok. When hot, add the pork and stir-fry for about 3 minutes or until just cooked through. Remove and set aside.

5. Add another tablespoon oil and sear the onion until it begins to brown. Add the garlic, ginger, hoisin, vinegar and soy. Simmer for about 1 minute.

6. Add the julienne mushrooms and the white button mushrooms, stock, snow peas, and cilantro. Return pork to the wok, stirring to combine, and add peppers.

7. To serve, spoon pork over steamed rice and garnish with sprinkling of cashews.

Serves 6 to 8

Rosé d'Anjou or white Zinfandel

Grilled Fish with Herbed Tomato Relish

Plump roma tomatoes, which don't need to be skinned and seeded, are the perfect choice for making this fresh-tasting accompaniment for any grilled fish. Remember to chop the herbs in the relish just before serving.

Ingredients

Relish

2	pounds roma tomatoes, chopped
3	tablespoons balsamic vinegar
2	large shallots, minced
1	clove garlic, minced
1/3	cup extra virgin olive oil
1	teaspoon sea salt
1	teaspoon freshly ground pepper
2	tablespoons chopped fresh basil
2	tablespoons chopped fresh thyme
1	tablespoon chopped fresh sage
2	tablespoons chopped fresh fennel sprigs
2	pounds firm-textured fish, such as Sea bass, halibut, or cod
	Additional olive oil, for basting

Method

1. In a glass or stainless bowl, combine the tomatoes, vinegar, shallots, garlic, oil, salt and pepper. Cover and set aside.

2. Lightly brush the fish on both sides with oil. Heat a grill, barbecue or cast iron pan to medium heat.

3. Arrange the fish on the grill and cook over medium heat, basting with olive oil as needed, for 2 to 3 minutes per side, turning once, or until the fish is cooked through and flakes with a fork.

4. Meanwhile, chop the fresh herbs just before serving. This releases the oils of the herbs and maximizes the fragrance of the relish. Add to the tomatoes, stirring to combine.

5. Serve the relish alongside the fish.

Serves 6 to 8

 Mills Reef Sauvignon Blanc

Pacific Coast Halibut Cheeks

Early spring brings my favorite fish to market —halibut, and better still, these moist and succulent morsels from behind the mouth.

Can fish be addicting? These are. They can be substituted in any of your recipes utilizing fish. I urge you to try them.

Ingredients

2 ¹/₂ pounds fresh halibut cheeks

¹/₃ cup unbleached all-purpose flour

2 tablespoons unsalted butter

2 tablespoons olive oil

3 shallots, finely minced

3 tablespoons flat-leaf parsley, chopped

2 teaspoons chopped fresh thyme

²/₃ cup white wine

Sea salt

Freshly ground white pepper

Method

1. Dredge the halibut cheeks in the flour.

2. Heat the oil and butter together in a fry pan, add the halibut cheeks cook until golden brown, about 2 to 3 minutes on each side. Add the shallots, parsley and thyme. Continue to cook for 4 more minutes.

3. Add the wine to the pan along with the salt and white pepper and cook until the cheeks are cooked through, depending on the size of the cheeks, maybe another minute or so.

4. Serve the cheeks with steamed young potatoes and ladle the pan juices over top.

Serves 6

 Dry Riesling

Tuna Fillets with Tapenade

Tapénade is a Provençal olive paste made with the tiny niçoise olives from the south of France. These olives have a wonderful fruity taste, however they are very small. You can substitue kalamata olives. The French use this paste to spread on baguettes; I have used it here to complement fresh tuna. Either way, enjoy. The flavor is truly marvelous.

Ingredients

2 to 3 pounds fresh tuna, ahi or yellowfin

Olive oil for frying

Sea salt

Freshly ground pepper

Sauce

Olive oil for rubbing the garlic

$^1/_2$ head garlic (about 4 to 5 cloves)

1   cup Greek or niçoise olives, pitted

2   tablespoons capers

2 to 3 anchovy fillets

1   teaspoon chopped fresh thyme
     or 1/2 teaspoon dried

2   tablespoons dark rum

4   tablespoons extra virgin olive oil

$^1/_2$ teaspoon fresh ground pepper

Method

1. Cut about 1/8 inch off the top of each garlic clove, rub the cloves all over with the olive oil, place in a garlic roaster or loosely wrap in tin foil. Place in a 325° oven and roast for 30 to 40 minutes, or until the garlic is soft and golden. Set aside.

2. Place the olives, capers, anchovy, thyme and peeled roasted garlic in the bowl of a food processor. Process until chunky, add the rum and olive oil and give it a few more pulses. Do not make it a complete purée. A little texture is nice. Taste for seasoning and add the pepper. Set aside.

3. Heat a cast iron fry pan to medium high heat. Lightly season the tuna with the sea salt and pepper. Sear the tuna in the hot pan for 1 minute on each side. Place in the oven for 10 to 15 minutes or until the tuna is cooked to your desired doneness.

4. To serve, place the tuna on your serving plate and top with a generous portion of tapénade.

Serves 6

 Hermitage

Fresh Sea Bass with Shallots, Chives & Cream

My choice for this dish is European or Chilean sea bass, which I'll admit is fairly pricey.

An alternative would be red snapper or true grey cod. The flavorful sauce makes an aristocrat of any fish.

Ingredients

2 ¹/₂ pounds fresh sea bass, red snapper or cod

2   tablespoons unsalted butter

4   large shallots, minced

1   cup fish stock

¹/₃   cup dry white table wine

¹/₂   cup heavy cream

3   tablespoons snipped chives

    Sea salt

    Freshly ground pepper

¹/₂   pound fresh shrimp

¹/₂   bunch fresh parsley, chopped

6   stems freshly snipped chives for garnish

Method

1. Heat the butter in a sauté pan, add the shallots and soften, taking care not to brown. Pour in the fish stock and the wine, bring to a slow simmer.

2. Gently slide in the pieces of fish, about 3 at a time so you do not crowd them. Poach the fish until it is cooked completely through, about 6 to 10 minutes, depending on the thickness. Remove from the pan with a slotted spoon and keep in a warmed oven.

3. Bring the poaching liquid to a boil and reduce it by half the original volume. Add the heavy cream and snipped chives and let the sauce simmer until it is thick enough to coat the back of a spoon. Adjust the flavors with salt and pepper. Turn the heat to low and add the shrimp meat to the pan. Cook for no more than 1 minute, just to warm the shrimp through.

4. Lay the poached fish on your serving plate, ladle a spoonful of the sauce over top of the fish, finish with a garnish of chopped parsley and snipped chives.

Serves 6

 Mills Reef Hawkes Bay Chardonnay

# Poached Salmon with Spinach & Vermouth Sauce

Fresh salmon from the Pacific Northwest is a real taste treat. Salmon lovers agree that grilled, baked,

poached or fried it is the ultimate west coast fish. Here is a recipe for poaching that I know you'll enjoy.

Ingredients

Sauce

1	large bunch fresh spinach, washed, stems removed
	Juice from 1/2 lemon
2/3	cup heavy cream
1 1/2	cups rich fish stock
2	tablespoons white vermouth
	Sea salt
	Freshly ground white pepper

Fish

6	8-ounce pieces skinned salmon fillet, 1 1/2 inches thick
3	cups fish stock
	Whole chive stems for garnish

Method

SAUCE

1. For the sauce, bring the 1 1/2 cups of stock to a boil, blanch the spinach leaves for 30 seconds in the stock. Remove the leaves with a slotted spoon.

2. Transfer the spinach to a food processor and purée with the lemon juice.

3. Bring the fish stock to a boil and reduce the volume by half. Add the vermouth, cream and pepper and bring the sauce to a simmer. As it begins to thicken stir in the spinach purée. Adjust the seasoning to taste. The sauce should be thick enough to coat the back of a spoon. This sauce can be made in advance and chilled until serving time.

FISH

4. To poach the fish, place the 3 cups of fish stock in a deep sided sauté pan. Bring the stock to a simmer, gently poach the fish pieces for about 5 to 7 minutes or until cooked through. Remove with a slotted spoon.

5. Arrange a piece of fish on a dinner plate and spoon some of the sauce over the top. Garnish with 2 fresh chive stems.

Serves 6

  Stags' Leap Winery Chardonnay

Marinated Salmon Fillet with Ginger

Using our fabulous west coast salmon, this recipe enhances the fresh fish flavor with

an Asian-style marinade using minced ginger, rice wine vinegar and sesame oil.

Ingredients

4   cloves garlic, minced

2   shallots, finely chopped

2   tablespoons rice wine vinegar

1   piece (about 3 inches) fresh ginger, minced

2   tablespoons sesame oil

$^1/_3$ cup soy sauce

1   salmon fillet (about 2 lbs. 1 to $^1/_2$ inches thick)

3   tablespoons peanut oil or corn oil

Method

1. Combine the garlic, shallots, vinegar, ginger, sesame oil and soy. Place the salmon in a shallow baking dish and pour over the marinade. Cover and refrigerate for 2 to 4 hours.

2. Heat the peanut oil in a heavy skillet. When the oil is hot, slide the fish into the pan, skin side down, and cook for 5 to 8 minutes until is is almost done. It should be barely opaque and springy to the touch.

3. Pour in the marinade and continue to cook the salmon for about 5 minutes longer, or until flaky in texture and cooked through.

4. Transfer the salmon to a serving platter and keep warm. Continue to reduce the sauce until it thickens. Spoon sauce over the top to serve.

Serves 6

  White Zinfandel

Cataplana

A cataplana is indispensable to a Potuguese kitchen. This clam-shaped copper steamer is not only the cooking vessel but the serving dish. When opened at the table it dramatically releases the fabulous aroma of what's inside. A large pot with a tight lid can be substituted. The traditional version of cataplana does not include mussels or prawns, but living on the west coast inspired me to add them for local flavor.

Ingredients

1/4   cup olive oil

2   medium yellow onions, diced

3   garlic cloves, minced

2   cups plum tomatoes, chopped

1   cup white wine

1   green pepper, diced

1   bunch fresh parsley, chopped

  Sea salt

  Freshly ground pepper

  Piri-piri sauce to taste or Tabasco

24   manila or littleneck clams in shells

24   mussels in shells

12   prawns in shells

1/4   cup brandy

1   chorizo sausage, sliced

6   cups cooked rice

Method

1. In a cataplana dish, heat the olive oil, add the onion and garlic, soften them but do not brown. Add the tomatoes, wine, green pepper, parsley, salt, pepper and piri piri sauce to taste.

2. Bring to a boil, stirring frequently. Add the shellfish and brandy, cover and cook for about 5 minutes. Discard any unopened shells. Meanwhile, fry the chopped chorizo until crisp. Set aside. Serve cataplana over rice with the chorizo as your garnish

Serves 6 to 8

 Douro or Bairrada red wine

Grilled Asian Scallops

These scallops can be successfully grilled indoors on a stovetop griller or on your barbecue.

If fresh shiitake or oyster mushrooms are available, they go very well with the scallops.

Ingredients

1   pound fresh sea scallops

1   bunch fresh spinach (washed, dried & stemmed)

8 to 10 dried Chinese mushrooms (soaked in warm water)

3   tablespoons hoisin sauce

1   tablespoon minced fresh ginger

2 to 3 garlic cloves, minced

2   tablespoons rice wine vinegar

3   tablespoons soy sauce

1 to 2 teaspoons sesame oil

1   tablespoon peanut oil

1   tablespoon piri-piri sauce or Thai chili sauce

Small red chilies for garnish

Oil for deep frying

Griddle for grilling

Method

1. Blot the scallops dry on kitchen towels. In a large bowl mix together the hoisin, ginger, garlic, vinegar, soy, sesame oil, peanut oil and piri-piri sauce. Toss in the scallops and coat them well with the mixture.

2. Let the scallops marinate for at least 30 minutes in this sauce.

3. Drain the mushrooms and cut off the woody stem. Heat the griddle and brush it with a little oil to prevent sticking. Place the scallops on the grill and quickly sear both sides. Dip the mushrooms in some of the excess marinade and grill them as well.

4. Heat the oil for deep frying and very quickly plunge the dry spinach leaves into the hot oil; they will immediately crisp up. Remove, drain on paper towels.

5. To serve, line a small appetizer plate or a shell plate with the fried spinach, place 3 to 4 scallops on top of the spinach as well as a grilled mushroom. Garnish with a red chili.

Serves 6 to 8

Black Bean Prawns

The sauce gets its intense flavor from Chinese black beans as well as garlic. I find the flavor almost addicting.

Use with the same sauce with chicken, if you prefer.

Ingredients

Marinade

6 to 8 whole cloves garlic

1   piece (about 5 inches) fresh ginger, peeled and cut into small pieces

$^1/_2$ cup Chinese fermented black beans

$^1/_3$ cup peanut oil

$^1/_4$ cup soy sauce

2   tablespoons sesame oil

1   tablespoon hot chili flakes

1 $^1/_2$ pounds raw prawns (30-32 count), heads removed

   Cilantro sprigs

   Sliced green onions

Method

1. Place the garlic and ginger pieces into a mini chopper or small food processor. Pulse until the mixture is puréed. Transfer to a bowl.

2. Coarsely chop the black beans (or pulse with the mini chopper a few times). Add the beans to the garlic mixture.

3. Pour in the peanut oil, soy sauce, sesame oil, and chili flakes, stirring to combine. The consistency should be that of thick barbecue sauce.

4. Peel the prawns, remove any visible intestines and butterfly them halfway up the back. Toss them with the black bean mixture, cover and set aside in the refrigerator for at least 30 minutes.

5. Heat about 1 tablespoon peanut oil in a large wok or frying pan over high heat. Add the prawns and the sauce and quickly stir-fry for 4 to 5 minutes or until they turn bright pink. Take care not overcook.

6. Transfer the prawns to a serving platter and garnish with the sprigs of cilantro or chopped green onion. Serve immediately.

Serves 6

 Shaftsbury Beer

Jose's Cracked Crab

My husband José is truly a fantastic cook; he prepares a lot of our family meals which I just love. I sit in our kitchen sipping wine and watch.   Being Portuguese, his specialty of course is fish. This is his version of westcoast crab done in his Portuguese style.

Ingredients

2	live Dungeness crabs, 2 to 3 pounds each
1/2	cup olive oil
4	large shallots, chopped
5 to 6	garlic cloves, minced
1	medium yellow onion, diced
1	bay leaf
1	tablespoon piri-piri sauce or Tabasco
1	cup white wine
2	teaspoons sea salt
1/2	bunch fresh cilantro, chopped

Method

1. Bring an 8-quart pot of water to the boil, plunge in the crabs and cook them for 6 minutes per pound. Remove the crabs from the water and run under cold water. When the crab is cool enough to handle, pull the top shell off and run the body under cold water. This will wash away all the internal waste.

2. Break the legs off , bend them in half and crack them open, so that the meat is exposed. Cut the body into quarters. Set aside all the pieces and prepare the sauce.

3. In a 3-quart pot, heat the olive oil, add the shallot, garlic, onion, bay leaf and piri-piri. Sauté until the onion begins to turn light golden brown.

4. Place all the cracked crab pieces in the pot and stir the pieces so they become coated with the onion mixture, cover and let the crab warm through for about 5 minutes stirring at 2-minute intervals. Pour in the wine, salt and cilantro, stir to combine and cover again for 3 minutes.

5. To serve, pour the entire amount into a large serving bowl. Give all your guests bibs, crab crackers and picks and lots of fresh crusty French bread. Enjoy

Serves 4 to 6

 Jean Durup, Château de Maligny Chablis Premier Cru

Prawns & Caperberries

José and I first discovered caperberries in Spain, and just knew that we had to bring them to Vancouver. Sure enough the entire city went crazy; people were buying jars of caperberries out of restaurants! My student wanted more reasons to use them with other foods, and so I created this recipe.

Ingredients

1   cup olive oil

1/3   cup balsamic vinegar

1/2   bunch parsley, chopped

2   bay leaves

2 to 3 garlic cloves, minced

1   tablespoon Dijon mustard

         Pinch sea salt & freshly ground pepper

1   pound raw headless tiger

         prawns, shelled

1   large onion

1/2   cup caperberries

1   1-pound package pasta of your choice

Method

1. In a large bowl combine the oil, vinegar, parsley, bay leaves, garlic, Dijon, salt & pepper. Stir to combine. Add the prawns and let marinate for about 20 minutes.

2. Slice the onion, heat a sauté pan, pour a little of the marinade into the pan, add the onion & cook until browned, add the bowl of prawns together with the marinade and cook until the prawns turn bright pink. Add the caperberries. Adjust the seasoning to taste.

3. Serve over pasta.

Serves 4

Californian Sauvignon Blanc, such as Duckhorn, Kunde or Merryvale

Shuckers Fried Squid

The way to a great chef's recipe is through his heart...his wife's that is! Kerry Sear, Exec Chef at the Four Seasons in Seattle

and wife Heidi are very good friends of mine. I was so happy Heidi was able to persuade him to share one of his creations for my book.

In my opinion, and a few others', it is the best calamari ever. Thank you Kerry.

Ingredients

2   pounds squid, cut in rings

2   cups milk

2   tablespoons garlic, chopped

1   teaspoon parsley, chopped

1   teaspoon thyme, chopped

1   teaspoon black peppercorns

1 2/3 cup flour

Salt

Pepper

Cheesecloth bag

Method

1. Place garlic, parsley, thyme and peppercorns into a cheese-cloth bag. Add to milk, then add cut squid and tentacles. Marinate for two days in the fridge.

2. Strain off the milk and roll the squid into seasoned flour. Tip: use a wire strainer or wire basket to remove excess flour.

3. Deep fry in hot oil at 375° until golden brown. Stir while the squid is cooking. Serve with cocktail sauce, lemon or garlic mayonnaise.

Serves 6

 Kunde Estate Chardonnay

Desserts

Fresh Banana Ice Cream

Mango Sorbet, Raspberry Sorbet & Kiwi Sorbet

Cold Lemon Soufflé

Crème Caramel

Pear & Mascarpone Cheese Tart

Frangipane with Cherries

Lemon Curd Tartlets

Flowers & Phyllo

Caren's Apple Flan

Fresh West Coast Plum Tart

Grand Marnier Soufflé

Mexican Chocolate Cake with Banana Sauce

Hazelnut Gâteau

Angel Cake with Pistachio Cream

Festive Christmas Stollen

Apple Strudel in Phyllo

Frozen Marbled Mousse

Chocolate Nut Torte

Coconut Macadamia Cookies

Decadent Chocolate Chunk Cookies

Georgia Pecan Cookies

Butter Cookies with White Chocolate and Pistachios

Fresh Banana Ice Cream

Take a look at this quick ice cream recipe that doesn't even require an ice cream maker.

As an accompaniment, serve a spoonful or two of warm chocolate sauce.

Ingredients

Ice Cream

4   very ripe bananas

1   cup heavy cream

$^1/_2$ cup half-and-half

2 to 3 tablespoons liqueur, such as
    Frangelico

Sauce

$^1/_2$ pound good-quality French chocolate

$^1/_3$ cup half-and-half

3 to 4 tablespoons liqueur, such as
    Frangelico

Method

1. For the ice cream, peel the bananas and cut into 2-inch pieces. Arrange them on a tray in a single layer and freeze for at least 3 hours or until solid.

2. Meanwhile, combine the heavy cream and the half-and-half.

3. When bananas are frozen, place the pieces into a food processor fitted with a metal blade. Pulse for 10 to 12 times just to break up the bananas. The consistency should be like coarse cornmeal.

4. With the machine running, slowly pour in the cream mixture, scraping down the sides of the bowl as needed, until the ice cream emulsifies. Add the liqueur.

5. Transfer to a bowl and serve immediately or cover and freeze for up to 4 days.

6. For the sauce, combine the chocolate, half-and-half and liqueur in the top of a double boiler over low heat. Stir constantly until the sauce is smooth and creamy. (This sauce keeps up to 1 week in the refrigerator.)

7. To serve, place ice cream in dessert bowls and pass the chocolate sauce at the table.

Serves 4 to 6

Pictured on page 142

Mango, Raspberry & Kiwi Sorbet

Vibrant color, intense flavor, no fat, no guilt -- these desserts have everything . . . except preservatives,

so make only the amount you'll need as this will serve about 6.

Ingredients

Simple Syrup

2 1/4 cups granulated sugar

2 cups water

Kiwi Sorbet

9 to 10 fresh large kiwis

4 teaspoons fresh lemon juice

1 1/2 cups simple syrup

Method

SIMPLE SYRUP

1. Combine the sugar and the water in a pot and boil until the sugar dissolves, about 1 minute. Cool and chill. Yields about 2 cups.

KIWI SORBET

2. Peel and mash the kiwis, place them in a food processor and pulse 10 to 15 times. Do not let the machine run or you will pulverize the black seeds and lose the gorgeous green of the fruit.

3. Mix the kiwi pulp with the lemon juice and 1 1/2 cups of the prepared simple syrup. Stir well to ensure the mixture is combined. Chill for 1 to 2 hours.

4. Place the mixture in an ice cream machine and follow the manufacturer's directions for use. The small hand-cranked models such as the Donvier work wonderfully. if you don't have an ice cream maker, pour the mixture into a pan and place in the freezer. When the mixture becomes slushy after 2 to 3 hours, mash with a fork to break up the ice crystals, then return to the freezer. Mash it again at 1-hour intervals until the mixture is firm.

5. When the sorbet is ready, serve or transfer to a bowl to keep for 4 to 7 days in the freezer.

Ingredients

Mango Sorbet

4   medium mangoes

4   tablespoons fresh lemon juice

1   cup simple syrup

Fresh Raspberry Sorbet

2   cups fresh raspberries

2   teaspoons lemon juice

1 $^1/_2$ cups simple syrup

Method

MANGO SORBET

2. Peel the mangoes and remove the large pit from the middle. Cut into pieces and place in the food processor along with the lemon juice. Purée until it is smooth.

3. Mix the mango purée with the sugar syrup and chill for 1 to 2 hours.

4. Follow the freezing directions on page 124 (step 4)

5. When the sorbet is ready, serve or transfer to a bowl to keep for 4 to 7 days in the freezer.

RASPBERRY SORBET

2. Place the raspberries in the food processor along with the lemon. Pulse the machine until the berries are smooth.

3. Stir in the simple syrup and chill the mixture for 1 to 2 hours.

4. Follow the freezing directions on page 124 (step 4)

5. When the sorbet is ready, serve or transfer to a bowl to keep for 4 to 7 days in the freezer.

Iced Lemon Souffle

Unlike cooked soufflés, which have a tendency to fall, the cold version will never collapse, which makes it an encouraging option. This refreshing dessert is light, not too sweet and easily prepared ahead of time — perfect after a big meal.

Ingredients

6   gelatin sheets or 1 envelope
      packaged gelatin

2   tablespoons water

$^1/_2$ cup lemon juice

$^3/_4$ cup granulated sugar

      Grated rind of 3 large lemons

8   large egg whites

1   cup heavy cream

$^1/_4$ cup granulated sugar

      Candied violets or candied mimosa and

      Fresh mint leaves for garnish

$^1/_4$ cup heavy cream, for garnish

      Parchment paper

1   quart soufflé dish

Method

1. If you like your soufflé to stand above the dish, cut a band of parchment paper that is the circumference of the dish by about 2 inches higher. Lightly oil it with a flavorless oil such as safflower. Wrap the band around the 1-quart soufflé dish and tape the ends securely. Set aside.

2. In a small pot combine the gelatin sheets and water. When it begins to soften add the lemon juice and continue to stir until the gelatin is completely dissolved. Add the sugar and rind and stir over very low heat until the sugar is dissolved. Chill the mixture for about 20 minutes. It should be slightly syrupy

3. Beat the egg whites until soft stiff peaks form. Slowly beat in the lemon syrup, and set aside. Beat the cream stiff with 1/4 cup of sugar. Quickly fold together the lemon/egg white mixture together with the beaten cream. Pour the mixture into the prepared dish and chill for at least 3 hours.

4. To garnish the soufflé, whip the remaining 1/4 cup of cream, place it in a piping bag fitted with a star tip and pipe rosettes on the top. Place the candied flowers on top of the rosettes together with fresh mint leaves. If you don't have candied flowers, use fresh slices of lemon with the mint leaves.

Serves 8

Creme Caramel

Most crème caramels are made with heavy cream as the custard base. In this recipe I use half-and-half combined with milk to give you a lighter version. The caramel is my favorite part of this dessert, so make lots.

Ingredients

Caramel

2 cups sugar

1 teaspoon fresh lemon juice

5 drops water

Custard

1 cup half-and-half

1 cup whole milk

1 whole vanilla bean

3 whole eggs

2 egg yolks

$^1/_2$ cup granulated sugar

6 individual ovenproof ramekins

Whipped cream, garnish

Candied violets, garnish

Method

CARAMEL

1. In a heavy bottomed saucepan or sugar boiler combine the sugar, lemon juice and water. Bring to a boil and continue to boil until the sugar begins to turn light amber, about 8 minutes. Turn the heat down and watch the sugar very carefully so that it does not burn. At this point it darkens very fast. It should be a nice caramel color.

2. Carefully pour the hot sugar into the ramekin dishes, rotating and turning the dish so that the caramel coats the sides of the dish evenly. Set aside until the caramel sets. Prepare the custard.

CUSTARD

3. Scald the milk, cream and vanilla bean together. Turn off the heat and let the mixture cool slightly. Preheat the oven to 350°.

4. While the milk is cooling, beat the whole eggs together with the yolks and the sugar, beating until the sugar is almost dissolved. Pour the hot milk into the eggs, gently whisking to incorporate. Be very careful not to incorporate any air into the milk or this will create holes in your custard. Strain the mixture through a fine-mesh sieve. Then pour it into the prepared dishes. Set the dishes in a pan of hot water (bain-marie). Bake for about 25 to 30 minutes or until a knife inserted into the middle of the custard comes out clean. Chill for several hours before serving.

5. Unmold onto a serving dish and garnish with whipped cream and candied violets.

Serves 6 to 8

Pear & Mascarpone Cheese Tart

While traveling in Italy, I discovered a store selling jars of miniature pears preserved in grappa syrup. I was so taken with their appearance that I brought them back to my cooking school and created this Italian tart featuring these tiny pears.

Ingredients

Pastry

1	cup unbleached all purpose flour
1/2	cup cold unsalted butter, cut into pieces
3	tablespoons icing sugar
1	tablespoon lemon rind finely grated

Filling

1	16 ounce jar miniature pears preserved in grappa or 5 small fresh pears
2/3	cup granulated sugar
8	ounces mascarpone cheese
1	egg
1/2	teaspoon pure vanilla extract
1/2	cup toasted chopped hazelnuts

Method

1. For the pastry, place the flour, butter, sugar and lemon in a bowl of a food processor fitted with a metal blade. Pulse 8 to 10 times, to break up the butter, and then continue to process until the dough leaves the sides of the bowl and forms a loose ball.

2. Wrap in plastic wrap and chill 15 minutes.

3. Preheat the oven to 400°. Remove dough from plastic and flatten slightly. Roll out onto a lightly floured surface to a thickness of 1/4 inch. Fit into a 9-inch tart pan with removable bottom. (If you find the pastry quite short and unable to roll easily, simply press it into the pan by hand; this will not affect the final result.)

4. Fit a sheet of parchment or waxed paper inside the shell and fill it with beans or pie weights. Blind bake the shell for 12 to 15 minutes. Remove and set aside to cool.

5. Meanwhile, peel and core the pears, if using fresh, and slice lengthwise into sixths. Sprinkle with the 1/3 cup sugar and set aside. (If using pears in grappa, drain and reserve the syrup and slice the pears in half. You do not need to use any sugar.)

6. In a large bowl combine the cheese, remaining 1/3 cup sugar, egg and vanilla. Spread the cheese mixture over the cooked pastry shell.

7. Arrange the pear slices (or halves) attractively over top and bake for 20 minutes or until the tart is golden brown. Just before serving, sprinkle on the hazelnuts, if desired.

Serves 6 to 8

 Kopke 1977 Porto Colheita

French Frangipane Tart

This baked almond-flavored tart has become a favorite of ours in the winter. I often serve it with preserved fruit,

such as brandied cherries or plums, but consider it for the summer as well, topped with your choice of seasonal fresh fruit.

Ingredients

Pastry

1	cup all-purpose flour
$^1/_2$	cup unsalted butter
3	tablespoons icing or confectioners' sugar
1	tablespoon ground almonds

Filling

1	cup whole blanched almonds
$^1/_2$	cup unsalted butter, at room temperature
$^1/_2$	cup granulated sugar
2	large eggs
1	tablespoon dark rum
1 to 2	cups fruit, such as brandied cherries, plums or pears
$^1/_2$	cup whipped cream, for garnish

Method

1. For the dough, combine the flour, butter, sugar and almonds in a food processor fitted with a metal blade. Pulse 10 to 12 times to combine the ingredients.

2. Process for about 1 minute or until a ball of dough is formed and it leaves the sides of the bowl.

3. Press the dough into a 10-inch French flan pan and chill in the freezer for about 15 minutes.

4. Meanwhile, preheat the oven to 400°. Bake the dough for about 10 minutes. Then remove and set aside to cool. Decrease oven temperature to 375°.

5. For the filling, place the almonds in a food processor fitted with a metal blade and process until they reach the consistency of cornmeal. Set aside.

6. Beat the butter until soft and fluffy using an electric mixer. Add the sugar and beat until combined. Add the eggs, one at a time, and continue to beat until combined. Stir in the reserved nuts and the rum.

7. Spoon mixture into baked dough and smooth top evenly with a metal spatula. Spoon fruit over the top and return to the oven for about 30 minutes or until golden.

8. Serve with a dollop of whipped cream.

Serves 8 to 10

emon Curd Tartlets

People seem to think of lemon curd as very old fashioned, but I love it despite its age.

I have used it here to fill mini tart shells. You can also use it for a large tart shell or spoon the curd onto pancakes or waffles.

Ingredients

Basic Pastry recipe see page 128

8   tablespoons unsalted butter, melted

3   egg yolks

1   cup granulated sugar

Pinch of sea salt

$^1/_3$ cup freshly squeezed lemon juice

3   whole eggs

2   teaspoons finely chopped lemon zest

1   cup heavy cream, whipped for garnish

Candied flowers, fresh edible flowers,

or fresh fruit, garnish

Method

1. Place the butter, yolks, sugar, salt, lemon juice. eggs and zest in the top of a double boiler.

2. Whisk over simmering heat until the curd is thick enough to coat the back of the spoon.

3. Cover and chill until ready to serve.

4. Preheat oven to 400°. Bake the pastry in small tartlet pans. You must line the tarts with parchment and fill with weights; this is called blind baking. After 6 minutes of baking, remove the weights and replace the tarts in the oven to cook the bottom completely, approximately 6 more minutes, or until the pastry is a golden brown. Remove from the oven and cool.

5. Remove the baked pastry shells from the tray, fill with lemon curd and top with candied violets, candied mimosa, fresh edible flowers or, simply, small berries.

Makes 16

lowers & Phyllo

Edible flowers are tucked inside thin sheets of layered phyllo, which are baked in muffin cups

and then filled with a luscious pistachio custard.

Ingredients

6   sheets phyllo pastry (thawed)

3/4 cup melted unsalted butter

1   cup edible flowers, such as:

Johnny-jump-ups, pansies, nasturtiums

etc. (Yellow, orange & bright pink colors

work the best.)

Baking forms such as hearts, muffin tins,

or any shape that you like.

Custard

2   cups whole milk

1   vanilla bean, split

3   tablespoons cornstarch

1/2 cup sugar

2   tablespoons flour

4   egg yolks

1   cup toasted ground pistachio nuts

Method

1. Lay a sheet of the phyllo on your work surface. Brush the top with butter lay one more sheet of phyllo on top. Brush the top with butter again. Lay the flowers evenly on top lightly pressing so they adhere to the dough. (Remove the tough stems from the flowers so they will not poke holes through the dough.) Lay the third piece of phyllo on top of the flowers, pressing lightly so they stick together. Butter the top. Preheat oven to 400°.

2. Cut the dough into pieces 1 inch larger than the diameter of your pan shape. Butter the inside of the tins and press the phyllo pieces gently inside. The edges should overhang to create a flower effect. Bake for 6 to 8 minutes or until golden brown.

3. These phyllo cups can be made 2 or 3 days ahead of time and kept in a dry place.

CUSTARD

4. Scald the milk with the split vanilla bean.

5. Mix the cornstarch, sugar and flour together, then slowly whisk it into the yolks. When the milk is scalded, slowly pour it into the yolk-mixture, whisking all the time. Pour the whole mixture back into the pot and on medium heat, whisk continually until the custard is thick.

6. Chill, fold in the pistachios.

7. Fill the phyllo cups with the custard and serve garnished with fruit or more flowers.

Makes up to 2 dozen (depends on size)

Caren's Apple Flan

I served this dessert at a dinner party in my home and was thrilled when one of our guests, Ruy Paes-Braga,

so enjoyed it that he asked for the recipe to include it on the menu at his hotel, The Four Seasons.

Ingredients

Crust

1/2	pound cold unsalted butter, cut into chunks
2	cups unbleached all-purpose flour
1/3	cup confectioner's or icing sugar

Filling

6	medium Golden Delicious apples
1/2	cup currants
1/4	cup almond liqueur
1/3	cup granulated sugar
1	tablespoon cornstarch
1	large egg
1/2	cup half-and-half or milk
1/2	cup pine nuts or slivered almonds

Method

1. Combine the currants with the liqueur and set aside to soak.

2. For the crust, place the butter, flour and sugar in a food processor fitted with a metal blade. Pulse a few times to break up the butter. Turn the machine on and let it run for about 1 minute or until the dough leaves the side of the bowl and forms a ball.

3. Divide the dough in half, shaping it into two balls. (Wrap and freeze one ball for future use.) Cover the second ball of dough with plastic wrap and chill for about 15 minutes before rolling.

4. Flatten the chilled ball of dough slightly and then roll it out on a floured surface to a thickness of about 1/4 inch. Press the dough into a 9-inch French flan pan with a removable bottom and place in the freezer for about 20 minutes.

5. Meanwhile, preheat the oven to 400°.

6. Peel and core the apples. Shred them in a food processor fitted with a shredding disk and set aside.

7. In a large bowl, whisk together the sugar, cornstarch, egg and milk. Add the shredded apples and the currants with their soaking liquid, stirring to combine.

8. Spoon the apple mixture into the frozen pastry shell and bake for 20 minutes. Reduce the oven temperature to 375°. Sprinkle the pine nuts over top of the flan and continue to bake for an additional 20 minutes or until the top turns golden brown. Serve with lightly sweetened whipped cream or ice cream, if desired.

Serves 8 to 10

 Late Harvest Muscat

Fresh West Coast Plum Tart

The ease of this fresh tart is that there is no form. The pastry is simply rolled out very thin, fresh plums on top,

a bit of sugar, and laid free-form on a baking sheet. You have a wonderful fresh-tasting dessert without a lot of work.

The pastry bakes up crispy and any leftovers are marvelous with morning coffee.

Ingredients

Paté Brisée

1 $^1/_4$ cups unbleached all purpose flour

  Pinch of salt

$^1/_4$ teaspoon granulated sugar

7 $^1/_2$ tablespoons cold unsalted butter

4 tablespoons cold water

Filling

3 tablespoons unsalted butter

$^1/_2$ cup granulated sugar

$^1/_2$ cup ground hazelnuts

4 soda biscuits, ground

1 pound fresh prune plums, stoned
  and halved

Method

1. In a large mixing bowl, sift together the flour, salt and sugar, and cut in the butter, keeping the size of the butter a little larger than peas. Add the water all at once, mixing the dough together as quickly as possible. Overworking the pastry makes it tough. Wrap the dough in plastic wrap and chill for 15 minutes.

2. For the filling, mix the sugar, butter, hazelnuts and soda biscuits together. Set aside.

3. Preheat the oven to 400°. Roll the dough out very thin, 12 inches wide and about 16 inches long and about 1/8 inch thick. Fold the dough in half to lift it onto a large flat baking sheet. Open the dough flat, sprinkle half of the sugar/hazelnut mixture on the bottom, and evenly distribute the plums in a layer, leaving a 2-inch border free. Sprinkle the remaining half of the sugar mixture over top. Dot with the butter. Fold the border back over the plums and bake the tart for about 1 hour and 10 minutes, or until the pastry is golden brown and the plums are cooked.

4. Serve warm with ice cream.

Serves 6

Grand Marnier Souffle

When a light dessert is called for, soufflés, hot or cold, are the perfect answer.

One thing—the company waits for the soufflé, the soufflé waits for no one! Serve it as soon as it is removed from the oven.

Ingredients

2   tablespoons unsalted butter

2 to 3 tablespoons granulated sugar

4   egg yolks

1/3   cup sugar

1/4   cup Grand Marnier

2   teaspoons grated orange rind

6   egg whites

1/4   teaspoon cream of tartar

Method

1. Preheat the oven to 425°. Butter and sugar 6 little white ramekin dishes or a 1-quart soufflé dish. Set the prepared dishes on a cookie sheet.

2. Place the yolks in the top of a double boiler, whisk in the sugar and beat until thick and pale in color, about 1 to 2 minutes. Add the Grand Marnier and rind and continue to whisk. Transfer the mixture to a bowl to cool.

3. Meanwhile, beat the whites with the cream of tartar until soft stiff peaks form. Be careful not to overbeat. When the yolk mixture is cool, fold in 1/4 of the whites to lighten it up, then fold in the remaining whites taking care not to deflate them.

4. Fill the prepared soufflé dishes about 3/4 full, place them on a cookie sheet and bake for 5 minutes. Turn the heat down to 400° and continue to bake for about 15 minutes or until the soufflés are puffed and golden in color. Serve immediately.

Serves 6

*M*exican Chocolate Cake with Roasted Banana Sauce

The chocolate cake is lightened with the addition of the the beaten egg whites. What makes this cake really tasty is the roasted

banana sauce. The combination of maple syrup and bourbon marries perfectly with the bananas.

Ingredients

1 $^1/_2$ cups cake flour

1   teaspoon baking soda

   Pinch of sea salt

6   tablespoons Dutch cocoa powder

2   eggs, separated

1   cup sugar, divided

$^1/_2$ cup buttermilk

$^1/_3$ cup vegetable oil

Sauce

4   ripe bananas

$^1/_4$ cup pure maple syrup

$^2/_3$ cup heavy cream

3   tablespoons bourbon or rye whiskey

Method

1. Preheat the oven to 350°. Line the bottom of a 10-inch springform pan with parchment paper, set aside. Sift the flour, soda, salt and cocoa together, set aside. Beat the yolks until they begin to pale, about 1 minute. Pour in 1/2 cup of the sugar and continue to beat until doubled in volume, 1 more minute.

2. Pour half of the buttermilk into the egg yolks along with half of the dry ingredients, beating after each addition. Repeat for the second half. Add the oil and beat well.

3. Beat the whites with the remaining 1/2 cup of sugar until soft peaks form. Do not overbeat. Fold the whites into the batter and pour this into the prepared springform pan. Bake at 350° for 25 minutes or until a toothpick inserted to the middle comes out clean. Cool.

4. To make the sauce, make small cuts about 2 inches long in the skin of the bananas. Place the whole bananas on a baking tray a roast in a 350° oven for 20 minutes. The skin will become completely black. Remove from the oven, cool and peel.

5. Place the bananas in a food processor together with the syrup, cream and bourbon. Process until you have a smooth, creamy sauce.

6. To serve, place a wedge of the cake on a plate and ladle the roasted banana sauce over. Additional sliced bananas go well.

Serves 8

Hazelnut Gateau

The praline preparation may scare you a bit but please give it a try. It really is as easy as boiling water, only with sugar in place. The end result is magnificent.

Ingredients

Cake

1	cup toasted ground hazelnuts
1	teaspoon baking powder
1/2	teaspoon sea salt
6	eggs, separated
3/4	cup granulated sugar
1/2	teaspoon pure vanilla extract
	Icing sugar
	Jelly roll pan or two 8" square or round
	Cake pans

Buttercream

2	egg yolks
2	tablespoons granulated sugar
1	teaspoon pure vanilla extract
3/4	cup unsalted butter
1/2	cup powdered praline
1/2	cup heavy cream, whipped

continued on page 137

Method

CAKE

1. Line the pans with parchment paper, or grease and flour the pans. Set aside. Preheat the oven to 350°. Mix the nuts, baking powder and salt together, set aside.

2. Beat the whites until they are stiff but not dry, set aside. Beat the yolks slowly adding the sugar a little at a time, beating until the volume is doubled. This will take about 7 minutes. Stir in the vanilla. Fold in the nut mixture, then take 1/4 of the white mixture and fold it into the batter, just to lighten it. Carefully fold in the remaining whites without deflating. Turn the mixture into your prepared pans and bake for 20 to 25 minutes. Invert edges and cut into even thirds lengthwise. Set aside.

BUTTERCREAM

3. Beat the yolks, sugar and vanilla until smooth and light in color. Add the butter 1 tablespoon at a time. Beat until all the butter is used and the mixture is light and fluffy. Fold in the praline powder. Use the buttercream between the cake layers and on the outside. Smooth or pipe the whipped cream all over the top and stick the shards of praline in the center.

Praline

2	cups hazelnuts
2 ½	cups sugar
½	cup water

Method

PRALINE

4. Butter a cookie sheet and set aside. Toast the nuts at 325° for 10 minutes. Rub the skins off. It is easiest to rub between a tea towel. Set aside.

5. Place the water and sugar in a very heavy bottomed sauce-pan or sugar boiler, boil until the mixture is light golden, or a candy thermometer reaches 250°. Add the nuts and continue to cook until the color is caramel. This will happen very fast, so watch it the entire time. Pour the mixture out onto the buttered tray and cool.

6. Break the praline into large chunks, take 1 cup of the smaller pieces, place in the food processor and grind it to a powder. Use as directed in the buttercream. Use the remaining big pieces for decoration.

Serves 8

 Full rich Madeira

Angel Cake with Pistachio Cream

I love this cake because you can serve it plain, and please your guests

who are watching their fat intake, or serve it as I like it, lavishly covered with toasted pistachio cream.

Ingredients

Cake

1 3/4 cup egg whites (about a dozen)

1 teaspoon cream of tartar

1/4 teaspoon fine sea salt

1 1/4 cups sifted cake flour

1 1/2 cups sifted granulated sugar

1 teaspoon vanilla extract

3/4 teaspoon fresh lemon juice

Cream

1 1/2 cups heavy cream, whipped

1/4 cup sifted icing sugar

2 tablespoons liqueur of your choice

1 cup shelled unsalted pistachio nuts

Method

CAKE

1. Scatter pistachios on a cookie sheet and bake in a 300° oven for about 20 minutes or until toasted. Grind in a food processor fitted with a metal blade. Set aside. Leave the oven on.

2. Meanwhile, beat the whites on medium speed until frothy. Add the salt and cream of tartar and continue to beat until soft peaks form. Do not overbeat!

3. Fold in the sugar, 2 tablespoons at a time, being very gentle so as not to deflate the mixture. Repeat the process with the flour, adding a few tablespoons at a time, and finally add the vanilla and lemon juice.

4. Pour the batter into an ungreased 10-inch tube pan. Bake for 1 hour and 10 minutes or until golden on top. Remove and invert the cake until cool.

CREAM

5. Beat the cream with the sugar until almost stiff. Add the liqueur and fold in the ground nuts. Set aside.

6. Slice the cake into 3 equal layers with a serrated knife. Spread each layer evenly with the pistachio cream. Frost the whole cake with the remaining cream.

7. To decorate, arrange fresh fruit or edible flowers on top and chill until serving.

Serves 10

Festive Christmas Stollen

While I have cooked many recipes on television, this is the only recipe I have prepared on radio!

My friend Vicki, host of CBC's The Gabereau Show, *wanted a holiday recipe with lots of noise and personality.*

We kneaded and thumped our way to a perfect Christmas stollen.

Ingredients

$^1/_2$ cup warm water

2   tablespoons dry yeast

2   teaspoons granulated sugar

$^1/_2$ cup unsalted butter

1   cup scalded milk

$^1/_2$ cup sugar

1   teaspoon salt

6   cups unbleached all-purpose flour

$^1/_4$ teaspoon ground mace

$^1/_4$ teaspoon ground nutmeg

2   eggs, lightly beaten

Grated rind of 1 lemon

$^1/_2$ cup brandy

$^1/_2$ cup currants

$^1/_2$ cup rum

$^1/_2$ cup raisins

$^1/_2$ cup candied peel

$^1/_2$ cup chopped dried apricots

Powdered sugar or icing

Method

1. Place 1/2 cup warm water in a bowl. Add the sugar, stirring to combine. Sprinkle the surface with yeast and let it rest for about 10 minutes or until the mixture begins to bubble.

2. Combine the scalded milk, butter, sugar and salt. Let the butter melt and then set aside to cool to lukewarm. Soak the raisins in the rum and set aside; soak the currants in the brandy and set aside.

3. Place 3 cups of the flour, the mace and the nutmeg into a large mixing bowl. Add in the milk-butter mixture and the proofed yeast. Stir well, creating a thick batter, and then add the beaten eggs and lemon rind.

4. Stir in the currants with the brandy, the raisins with the rum, the candied peel and apricots, mixing to combine.

5. Add the remaining flour, 1 cup at a time, until blended. Turn the dough out onto a floured surface and knead for about 10 minutes until you have a nice smooth, elastic texture. If the dough is sticky, you may need to knead in a little more flour.

6. Place the dough in a lightly oiled bowl, cover with a kitchen towel and place in a warm, draft-free location for 1 to 1 1/2 hours or until doubled in size.

7. Preheat the oven to 350°. Punch the dough down and turn out onto a work surface. Shape it into wreaths, stollen-shaped loaf or braids.

8. Place in a warm, draft-free location and let it rise a second time for an additional 1 to 1 1/2 hours or until doubled in size. Bake for 40 minutes.

9. To serve, remove from the oven and dust with powdered sugar or thin icing.

Sauternes

Apple Strudel in Phyllo

Cosy up to the fire with a steaming slice of this easy-to-make strudel (à la mode, of course) and a full-roasted cup of coffee!

The phyllo pastry is available in the freezer section of most grocery stores or specialty Greek grocery stores.

Ingredients

6   apples (Golden, Granny Smith or Rome Beauties)

$^1/_2$ to $^3/_4$ cup granulated sugar

2   teaspoons cinnamon

$^1/_2$ cup raisins

$^1/_2$ cup toasted chopped almonds

4   soda biscuits, crumbled

1   package phyllo pastry

Approximately $^1/_2$ pound melted unsalted butter for brushing the pastry

Method

1. Let the phyllo thaw in the refrigerator overnight if possible.

2. Peel, core and slice the apples. Place in a non-aluminum pot together with the sugar, cinnamon and raisins. Simmer over medium heat until they are cooked through, but not mushy, about 15 minutes. Remove from heat and let cool.

3. Open the phyllo and lay it flat. Brush the first sheet with melted butter. Lay a second sheet on top and brush with butter again. Repeat with 7 sheets in all. Wrap and reserve the remaining phyllo.

4. Spoon the cooled apple mixture lengthwise in one long line on the pastry. Sprinkle the almonds on top, and finish with the crumbled soda biscuits.

5. Roll the strudel up jelly-roll fashion and secure the ends by folding them under. Brush the top with melted butter and score the top of the strudel with a sharp knife, barely cutting through the top two layers of dough.

6. Bake at 375° for 20 to 30 minutes or until the pastry is golden brown. Serve with ice cream or caramel sauce.

Serves 8 generously

Pear & Mascarpone Cheese Tart (page 128)

Fresh Fruit Sorbets (page 123) & Macadamia Nut Cookies (page 148)

Dark & White Chocolate Nut Torte (page 146)

Lemon Curd Tartlets (page 130)

Frozen Marbled Chocolate Mousse

Here's one of the easiest, most impressive desserts I teach. It's a chocoholic's dream and the ingredients are simple—white and dark chocolate and some heavy cream. You will need two 4 $^1/_2$ by -8 $^1/_2$-inch pans lined with parchment.

Ingredients

Light Mousse

6	ounces good white chocolate
$^1/_3$	cup milk
2	egg whites
I	cup heavy cream

Dark Mousse

8	ounces good semi sweet chocolate
2	tablespoons unsalted butter
$^1/_4$	cup water
5	large eggs, separated
I	cup heavy cream
	Fresh fruit or fruit purée sauce

Method

LIGHT MOUSSE

1. For light mousse, place the chocolate and milk in the top of a double boiler over medium heat. Stir until smooth and melted. Remove from the heat and whisk in the yolks, one at a time, whisking well after each addition.

2. Meanwhile, beat the whites until firm peaks form. Set aside. Whip the cream until stiff. Gently fold cooled chocolate, whipped cream and egg whites together. Set mixture aside.

DARK MOUSSE

3. For the dark mousse, place the chocolate, butter and water in the top of a double boiler over medium heat. Stir until smooth and melted. Remove from heat and whisk in the yolks, one at a time, whisking well after each addition.

4. Beat the egg whites until firm peaks form and set aside. Whip the cream until stiff. Fold 1/4 of the beaten whites into the chocolate to lighten the mixture. Gently fold in the remaining whites and whipped cream until the mousse is uniform in color.

5. In a shallow bowl, very gently swirl the two mousses together, creating a marbling effect. Pour the marbled mousse into prepared pans and freeze until set.

6. To serve, invert the mousse onto a serving platter and garnish with sliced seasonal fruit or serve with your favorite fruit sauce.

Serves 8 to 10

Dark & White Chocolate Nut Torte

This dessert not only looks spectacular and tastes great, but is simple to make.

Bake the torte using a traditional deep-sided cake pan or with a heart-shaped pan, as pictured.

Ingredients

Cake

1 $\frac{1}{4}$ cups hazelnuts

$\frac{3}{4}$ cup pistachio nuts

1 cup plus 2 tablespoons
   granulated sugar

4 eggs

1 tablespoon hot water

2 tablespoons unbleached flour

$\frac{1}{4}$ teaspoon baking powder

$\frac{1}{4}$ teaspoon sea salt

   Pinch of cream of tartar

continued on page 147

Method

CAKE

1. Grease and flour two 9-inch cake pans and set aside. Preheat the oven to 300°.

2. Place the hazelnuts and the pistachio nuts into a food processor fitted with a metal blade. Add 2 tablespoons of the sugar and pulse until the nuts are ground. Transfer the ground nuts to a cookie sheet and bake in the oven for 15 to 20 minutes or until toasted. Remove, cool and set aside.

3. Increase the oven temperature to 350°. Crack and separate the eggs, placing the yolks in a mixing bowl and the whites in a separate large bowl. Beat the yolks on high speed for about 3 minutes. Add the hot water and continue to beat for another minute.

4. Slowly pour in 3/4 cup of the remaining sugar and continue to beat until the mixture is thick and pale yellow in color.

5. Sift the flour, baking powder and salt together and add to the egg mixture, folding until incorporated.

6. Beat the egg whites until foamy. As soon as they begin to foam, add the cream of tartar and beat until soft peaks form. Add the remaining 1/4 cup of sugar and continue to beat just until the peaks can stand alone. Be careful not to overbeat them.

7. Stir the nuts into the yolk mixture. Take about 1/4 of the beaten egg whites and stir into the yolks to lighten the mixture. Then gently fold in the remaining whites, taking care not to overmix.

8. Pour the batter into the prepared pans and bake for about 20 minutes or until a toothpick inserted into the center comes out clean. Remove and invert onto cake racks to cool.

Ingredients

Buttercream

$1/2$	cup unsalted butter, room temperature
2	cups sifted icing sugar
1	teaspoon ground espresso dissolved in 2 tablespoons hot water

Chocolate Band

4	ounces French chocolate, melted
	Parchment paper
1	piece (about 4 ounces) white chocolate

Method

BUTTERCREAM

9. For the buttercream, beat the butter until soft. Add the sugar and dissolved espresso, beating until the buttercream is light and fluffy. Set aside.

CHOCOLATE BAND

10. For the chocolate band, measure the circumference of the cake and add 2 inches. Using that measurement, cut a piece of parchment paper that length by 4 inches wide. Using a metal spatula, spread the melted chocolate along the paper, covering it completely but leaving the 1-inch ends uncovered and free for handling.

11. Set aside for about 10 minutes until the chocolate is barely firm but not brittle. Meanwhile, lightly spread the buttercream between the layers of the cake and around the outside edges.

12. Carefully wrap the chocolate band (still attached to the parchment) around the outside of the cake; there should be a ridge about an inch over on the top, depending on the height of your cake. Chill the cake to set the chocolate. Then, carefully peel off the parchment, exposing the chocolate band.

13. Using a potato peeler, shave curls from the piece of white chocolate, mound the curls on the top of the cake, spreading them out evenly to cover completely. The more you use, the more decadent the cake!

Serves 8 to 10

 Kopke Ruby Porto

Coconut Macadamia Nut Cookies

These are as heavenly as they sound!

Ingredients

1   cup margarine (not the soft spreadable kind)

3/4   cup granulated sugar

1   teaspoon pure vanilla extract

1   egg, lightly beaten

2   cups unbleached all-purpose flour

1   teaspoon baking powder

1/4   cup good quality semisweet chocolate, (chopped)

1/2   cup chopped macadamia nuts

1/2   cup unsweetened long-thread coconut

Waxed paper

Parchment paper (cookie sheet lining)

Method

1. Preheat the oven to 375°. Line 2 cookie sheets with parchment paper, set aside. Beat the margarine, sugar and vanilla together in a mixing bowl. Beat on medium speed until light and fluffy, about 5 minutes. Add the egg. Combine to mix in. Stir in the flour, baking powder, chocolate and nuts. Mix to combine well.

2. Divide the dough in half and roll each half into a round cylinder 2 to 3 inches thick, depending on how big you like your cookies. Lay the sheet of waxed paper on your work surface, sprinkle the coconut on the paper and roll the cookie cylinder evenly in the coconut. Wrap the cylinders in paper or plastic wrap and chill for 30 minutes.

3. Cut the cylinders into 1/2-inch discs and place on the cookie sheets. Bake for about 15 minutes or until golden in color.

Makes 2 to 3 dozen

Decadent Chocolate Chunk Cookies

I have added oatmeal to these totally awesome double French chocolate cookies for no other reason than to appease the minimal (if any)

guilt that may be associated with consuming the best darn chocolate-oatmeal-coconut cookie you've ever eaten.

Ingredients

8   tablespoons unsalted butter

$^1/_4$ cup white sugar

$^1/_4$ cup brown sugar

1   egg

1   teaspoon pure vanilla extract

$^3/_4$ cup unbleached all-purpose flour

$^1/_2$ teaspoon baking powder

$^1/_2$ teaspoon sea salt

$^1/_2$ cup chopped nuts (walnuts,

       pecans, or your choice)

$^2/_3$ cup shredded coconut

1 $^1/_2$ cups good quality chocolate, chopped

$^1/_4$ cup rolled oats

Method

1. Preheat the oven to 350°. Beat the butter together with both the white and brown sugars until fluffy, about 5 minutes. Add the egg and vanilla and beat until mixed. Sift together the flour, baking powder and salt. Mix it into the batter along with the nuts, coconut, chocolate and rolled oats. Beat to incorporate the ingredients evenly.

2. Chill the batter for at least 3 hours. Using an ice cream scoop or large soup spoon, scoop even portions of batter onto a greased and floured cookie sheet.

3. Bake for 15 to 20 minutes or until golden in color.

Makes 30 to 36

Georgia Pecan Cookies

The State of Georgia in the U.S. is the world's most prolific pecan grower, which is the main reason I specify their regional specialty in this recipe. I invite you to close your eyes and enjoy a taste of the deep South with every mouthful!

Ingredients

1   cup unsalted butter

$^1/_3$ cup granulated sugar

2   teaspoons pure vanilla extract

2   teaspoons water

2   cups unbleached all-purpose flour

1   cup chopped Georgia pecans

    Icing sugar for dusting cookies

Method

1. Preheat oven to 325°. Line 2 cookie sheets with parchment paper.

2. Cream together the butter, sugar, vanilla and water.

3. Stir in the flour and then the pecans, mixing until the dough is smooth and holds together. Take about 1 tablespoon of dough and roll between your hands to form balls or fingers.

4. Space them evenly apart on the lined cookie sheet and bake for 20 to 25 minutes. Cool and dust with the icing sugar.

Makes 24 to 30

Butter Cookies with White Chocolate & Pistachios

These little butter cookies are made extra special by dipping one end of the cookie in chocolate and then in the toasted chopped pistachios. I urge you to make a double batch, because the minute you start dipping them in chocolate they disappear like magic.

Ingredients

1	cup unsalted butter, softened
$^1/_2$	cup icing sugar
$^1/_2$	teaspoon pure vanilla extract
1 $^1/_2$	cups unbleached all-purpose flour
4	ounces good white chocolate
1	cup pistachio nuts, toasted and chopped

Piping bag

Large star tube

Method

1. Cream the butter until soft, add the sugar and beat until light and fluffy. Add the vanilla and the flour and beat until the mixture is combined.

2. Preheat the oven to 375°. Place the mixture in a large piping bag fitted with a large star tube. Pipe the dough onto a cookie sheet into about 2 -inch lengths. Bake for 10 minutes, or until the cookies are light golden brown. Cool.

3. Melt the chocolate in a double boiler, dip one end of the cooled cookie into the chocolate, then immediately roll into the chopped pistachios. Lay the cookies on a flat surface until the chocolate sets.

Makes 36

Metric Equivalent Chart

WEIGHT

Metric	Imperial
15g	$\frac{1}{2}$oz
20g	$\frac{3}{4}$oz
25g	1oz
40g	$1\frac{1}{2}$oz
50g	2oz
75g	3oz
100g	4oz ($\frac{1}{4}$lb)
150g	5oz
175g	6oz
200g	7oz
225g	8oz ($\frac{1}{2}$lb)
250g	9oz
275g	10oz
300g	11oz
350g	12oz ($\frac{3}{4}$lb)
375g	13oz
400g	14oz
425g	15oz
450g	16oz (1lb)
900-1000g	2lb
$1\frac{1}{2}$kg	3lb
2kg	4lb
$2\frac{1}{2}$kg	5lb
3kg	6lb
$3\frac{1}{2}$kg	7lb
4kg	8lb

VOLUME

Metric	US Cup
50ml	$\frac{1}{4}$
75ml	$\frac{1}{3}$
100ml	$\frac{1}{2}$
150ml	$\frac{5}{8}$
200ml	$\frac{3}{4}$
225ml	1
275ml	$1\frac{1}{8}$
300ml	$1\frac{1}{4}$
400ml	$1\frac{3}{4}$
	2 = 1 pint (US)
750ml	3

LINEAR MEASURE

Metric	Imperial
3mm	$\frac{1}{8}$in
5mm	$\frac{1}{4}$in
1cm	$\frac{1}{2}$in
2.5cm	1in
4cm	$1\frac{1}{2}$in
5cm	2in
6.5cm	$2\frac{1}{2}$in
7.5cm	3in
10cm	4in
12.5cm	5in
15cm	6in
18cm	7in
20cm	8in
23cm	9in
25cm	10in
30cm	12in (1ft)
35cm	14in
38cm	15in
45cm	18in
60cm	24in
92cm	36in

SPOONS

Metric	Imperial
1.5ml	$\frac{1}{4}$ teaspoon
2.5ml	$\frac{1}{2}$ teaspoon
5ml	1 teaspoon
15ml	1 tablespoon
30ml	2 tbsp (1fl oz)
3 tsp	1 tablespoon
2 tbsp	1 fl oz
16 tbsp	1 cup (US)

OVEN TEMPERATURES

°C	°F Mark
110	225
130	250
140	275
150	300

Table of Substitutions and/or Equivalents

For 1 envelope dehydrated or dry yeast, use 1 cake compressed yeast.

For 1 cup granulated sugar, use 1 1/3 cups brown sugar.

For 1 cup honey, use 1 cup corn syrup.

For 1 cup sugar, use 1 cup molasses plus 1/4 to 1/2 teaspoon soda less 1/4 cup liquid in recipe.

For 1 teaspoon baking powder, use 1/2 teaspoon cream of tartar plus 1/4 teaspoon soda.

For 1 cup sour milk, use 1 cup buttermilk or 1 tablespoon lemon juice or vinegar plus sweet milk to make 1 cup.

For 1 square (1 ounce) unsweetened chocolate, use 3 to 4 tablespoons cocoa plus 1 1/2 teaspoons fat.

For 1 whole egg, use 2 egg yolks.

For 1 cup sifted all-purpose flour, use 1 cup plus 2 tablespoons sifted cake or pastry flour.

For 1 cup self-rising flour, use 1 cup all-purpose flour plus baking powder and salt.

For 1 cup liquid honey, use 1 to 1 1/4 cups sugar plus 1/4 cup liquid.

For juice of 1 lemon, use 3 to 4 tablespoons.

For 1 tablespoon cornstarch (for thickening), use 2 tablespoons flour or 4 teaspoons quick-cooking tapioca.

Index

A

Ancho chili dressing, rice & black bean salad, 51
Angel cake with pistachio cream, 138
APPETIZERS
  Blue corn fritters, 22
  Chicken satay, 27
  Corn cakes & grilled scallops with red pepper sauce, 23
  Crab cakes with avocado-papaya salsa, 24, 36
  Grilled zucchini rolls, 19
  Herbed cheese appetizers, 18
  José's herbed olives, 15
  Layered mascarpone torta, 17
  Marinated lamb on rosemary skewers, 26
  Prosciutto-Parmesan fingers, 20
  Quesadillas with black bean salsa, 21
  Santa Fe chicken, 25
  Tapénade, 112
  Tomato crostini, 35, 37
  Warm chèvre spread with toasted baguette, 16
Apple, cress & endive salad, 49
Apple flan, Caren's, 132
Apple strudel in phyllo, 140
Arborio rice, about, 8
Artichoke, fresh, pizza, 60, 71
Artichokes, with rolled Italian beef roast, 101
Arugula, about, 8
Asiago cheese, about, 8
Asian pasta with black sesame seeds, 64, 69
Asian scallops, grilled, 117
Asian vegetable & noodle salad with ginger dressing, 52
Avocado-papaya salsa, with crab cakes, 24, 36

B

Baked Portuguese-style chicken, 91
Balsamic vinegar, about, 8
Banana, fresh, ice cream, 123
Banana, roasted, sauce, with Mexican chocolate cake, 127
Basil-olive bread, 58
BEANS AND LEGUMES
  Beans, dried, and legumes, about, 10
  Black bean and rice salad with ancho chili dressing, 51
  Black bean prawns, 118
  Black bean salsa, with quesadillas, 21
  Fermented black beans, about, 11
  New wave niçoise salad, with green beans, 33, 42
  Northern Italian bean salad, 50
  Turkey and turtle bean chili, 92
  Tuscan bean soup with tomato crostini, 35, 37
  Vegetable and lentil soup, 38
Beef roast, rolled Italian, with artichokes, 101
Beets with chèvre, 34, 45
Black bean & rice salad, with ancho chili dressing, 51
Black bean prawns, 118
Black pasta with smoked salmon, 72, 73
Black sesame seeds, about, 8
Black sesame seeds, with Asian pasta, 64, 69

Bloody gazpacho, 28
Blue corn flour, about, 8
Blue corn fritters, 22
Blue cornmeal chicken with tomatillo salsa, 88, 108
Bocconcini, about, 9
Bouillon powder, about, 9
BREADS
  Baguette, toasted, with warm chèvre spread, 16
  Bread bowls, with spinach salad, 46
  Crostini, tomato, with Tuscan bean soup, 37
  Croutons, herbed garlic, with Caesar salad, 43
  Focaccia, classic, 56
  Mini calzones, 63
  Muffuletta, 59
  Olive-basil bread, 58
  Pizza dough, 60
  Sun-dried tomato bread, 57
BREADS, PIZZA & PASTA, 55-85
Brie, with roasted chicken, pizza, 62
Burgers, ginger sesame chicken, 89
Butter cookies with white chocolate & pistachios, 151

C

Caesar salad with herbed garlic croutons, 43
CAKES AND TORTES
  Angel cake with pistachio cream, 138
  Christmas stollen, 139
  Dark and white chocolate nut torte, 146
  Hazelnut gâteau, 136
  Mexican chocolate cake with roasted banana sauce, 127
Calzones, mini, 63
Caperberries, about, 9
Caperberries, with prawns, 120
Caperberries, in smoked salmon with black pasta, 73
Capers, about, 9
Caramelized onions & roasted chestnuts, with veal chops, 98
Caren's Apple Flan, 123
Caren's Pepper Steak with Oven Fries, 100, 105
Cashew & pork stir-fry, 109
Cataplana, 106, 116
Celery & Stilton Soup, 30
Celery root, about, 9
Celery root salad, 44
CHEESE
  Asiago, about, 8
  Beets with chèvre, 34, 45
  Bocconcini, about, 9
  Celery and Stilton soup, 30
  Chèvre, about, 9
  Farfalle with Italian sausage and radicchio, 75
  Gorgonzola and pine nut pizza, 61
  Herbed cheese appetizers, 18
  Layered mascarpone torta, 17
  Mascarpone, about, 12
  Mini calzone, 63
  Muffuletta, 59
  Pear and mascarpone cheese tart, 128, 141
  Prosciutto-Parmesan fingers, 20

Risotto croquettes, 84
Risotto with fennel, 83
Roasted chicken with Brie pizza, 62
Vegetarian lasagna, 80
Warm chèvre spread with toasted baguette, 16
Cherries, sun-dried, with grilled quail, 94
Chestnuts, roasted & caramelized onions, with veal chops, 98
Chèvre, about, 9
Chèvre spread, warm, with toasted baguette, 16
Chèvre with beets, 34, 45
CHICKEN
Baked Portuguese-style chicken, 91
Blue cornmeal chicken with tomatillo salsa, 88, 108
Chicken Provençal with wild mushrooms, 90
Chicken satay, 27
French roasted free-range chicken, 87
Ginger sesame chicken burgers, 89
Roasted chicken lasagna with wild mushrooms, 80
Roasted chicken salad with tropical salsa, 54
Roasted chicken with Brie pizza, 62
Santa Fe chicken, 25
Chili, turkey & turtle bean, 92
Chinese mushrooms, about, 9
Chocolate, about, 9
Chocolate cake, Mexican, with roasted banana sauce, 127
Chocolate chunk cookies, decadent, 149
Chocolate soufflé, hot, 127
Chocolate, white & dark, nut torte, 143, 146
Chocolate, white, & pistachios, with butter cookies, 151
Chorizo & tortellini soup, 39
Classic focaccia, 56
Classic Italian sauce, with gnocchi, 78
Coconut macadamia nut cookies, 142, 148
Cold duck pasta salad, 53
Cookies, Georgia pecan, 150
Cookies, butter, with white chocolate & pistachios, 151
Cookies, coconut macadamia nut, 148
Cookies, decadent chocolate chunk, 149
CORN AND CORNMEAL
Blue corn fritters, 22
Blue cornmeal chicken with tomatillo salsa, 88, 108
Grilled polenta with summer ratatouille, 82
Creamy polenta, 81
Corn cakes & grilled scallops with red pepper sauce, 23
Crab cakes, west coast, with avocado-papaya salsa, 24, 36
Crab, cracked, José's, 119
Creamy garlic dressing, 41
Creamy polenta, 81
Cress, apple & endive salad, 49
Crisp iceberg with roasted garlic dressing, 48
Croquettes, risotto, 84
Crostini, about, 10
Crostini, tomato, with Tuscan bean soup, 35, 37
Croutons, herbed garlic, with Caesar salad, 43
Crystallized flowers, about, 10
Curry, lamb, Indian, 102
Custard, with flowers in phyllo, 131

Dark & white chocolate nut torte, 143, 146
Decadent chocolate chunk cookies, 149
Demi-glace with veal scallops, 96
DESSERTS, 122-151
Dried wild mushrooms, about, 10

DRESSINGS, see Salads and Dressings
Duck breast with green peppercorn & mustard sauce, 95
Duck, cold, pasta salad, 53
Dutch processed cocoa, about, 10

Edible flowers, about, 10
Endive, about, 10
Endive, cress & apple salad, 49
ENTREES, 86-121
Extra virgin olive oil, about, 10

Farfalle with Italian sausage & radicchio, 75
Fennel, with risotto, 83
Fermented black beans, about, 11
Fiddlehead & Spinach Soup, 29
Fiddleheads, about, 11
Field Greens with Asian dressing, 41
FISH AND SHELLFISH
Black bean prawns, 118
Cataplana, 106, 116
Corn cakes & grilled scallops with red pepper sauce, 14
Fish sauce, about, 11
Fresh sea bass with shallots, chives & cream, 113
Grilled Asian scallops, 117
Grilled fish with herbed tomato relish, 110
José's cracked crab, 119
Marinated salmon fillet with ginger, 115
New wave niçoise, 33, 42
Pacific coast halibut cheeks, 111
Poached salmon with spinach & vermouth sauce, 107, 114
Prawns and caperberries, 120
Provençal seafood soup, 31
Shrimp wonton soup, 32
Shrimp-filled wonton ravioli with saffron sauce, 74
Shuckers fried squid, 121
Smoked salmon with black pasta, 73
Tuna with tapénade, 112
Turkey tonnato, 93
West coast crab cakes, 24
Five-blend peppercorns, about, 11
Flan, Caren's apple, 132
Flowers & phyllo, 131
Flowers, edible, about, 10
Focaccia, classic, 56
French frangipane tart, 129
French roasted free-range chicken, 87
Fresh artichoke pizza, 60, 71
Fresh banana ice cream, 123
Fresh pumpkin soup with toasted hazelnuts, 40
Fresh west coast plum tart, 133
Fried squid, Shuckers, 121
Fries, oven, with Caren's pepper steak, 100, 105
Fritters, blue corn, 22
Frozen marbled mousse, 145

Garlic croutons, herbed, with Caesar salad, 43
Garlic dressing, creamy, 41
Garlic, roasted, dressing, with crisp iceberg lettuce, 48

Gâteau, hazelnut, 136
Gazpacho, 28
Gelatin sheets, about, 11
Georgia pecan cookies, 150
Ginger dressing, with Asian vegetable & noodle salad, 52
Ginger sesame chicken burgers, 89
Ginger, with marinated salmon fillet, 115
GLOSSARY, 8-13
Gnocchi with classic Italian sauce, 78
Gorgonzola & pine nut pizza, 61
Grand Marnier soufflé, 134
Greek olives, about, 11
Green peppercorn & mustard sauce, with duck breast, 95
Greens, field, with Asian dressing, 41
GRILLING AND BARBECUING
    Chicken satay, 27
    Grilled Asian scallops, 117
    Grilled fish with herbed tomato relish, 110
    Grilled polenta with summer ratatouille, 82
    Grilled quail with sun-dried cherries, 94
    Grilled scallops & corn cakes with red pepper sauce, 23
    Grilled zucchini rolls, 19
    Herb crusted lamb chops, 104
    Marinated lamb on rosemary skewers, 26

Halibut cheeks, Pacific coast, 111
Hazelnut gâteau, 136
Hazelnuts, toasted, with fresh pumpkin soup, 40
Hearty vegetable lasagna, 76
Herb-crusted lamb chops, 104
Herbed cheese appetizers, 18
Herbed olives, José's, 15
Herbed tomato relish, with grilled fish, 110
Herbs and spices, storage, about, 11
Hot chocolate soufflé, 127

Ice cream, fresh banana, 123
Iceberg lettuce, crisp, with roasted garlic dressing, 48
Iced lemon soufflé, 126
Icing sugar, 11
Indian lamb curry, 102
Italian beef roast, rolled, with artichokes, 101
Italian sauce, classic, with gnocchi, 78
Italian sausage & radicchio, with farfalle, 75

José's cracked crab, 119
José's herbed olives, 15

Kalamata olives, about, 11
Kiwi sorbet, 124, 142

Lamb chops, herb crusted, 104

Lamb curry, Indian, 102
Lamb, leg of, with shiitake mushrooms & roasted garlic, 103
Lamb, marinated, with rosemary skewers, 26
Lasagna, hearty vegetable, 76
Lasagna, roasted chicken, with wild mushrooms, 80
Layered mascarpone torta, 17
Leg of lamb with shiitake mushrooms & roasted garlic, 103
Lemon curd tartlets, 130, 144
Lemon soufflé, iced, 126
Lentil & vegetable soup, 38

Macadamia nut coconut cookies, 148
Mango sorbet, 125, 142
Marbled mousse, frozen, 145
Marinated lamb on rosemary skewers, 26
Marinated salmon fillet with ginger, 115
Mascarpone, about, 12
Mascarpone cheese & pear tart, 128, 141
Mascarpone, layered torta, 17
Mexican chocolate cake with roasted banana sauce, 127
Mini calzones, 63
Mixed mushroom pasta, 65
Mousse, frozen marbled, 145
Muffuletta, 59
MUSHROOMS
    Asian pasta with black sesame seeds, 64
    Chicken Provençal with wild mushrooms, 90
    Cold duck pasta salad, 53
    Dried wild mushrooms, about, 10
    Grilled Asian scallops, 117
    Mixed mushroom pasta, 65
    Pork & cashew stir-fry, 109
    Spinach salad in bread bowls, 46
    Vegetable and lentil soup, 38
    Wild mushrooms with roasted chicken lasagna, 80
    Wild rice with sultana raisins & shiitake mushrooms, 85
Mustard & green peppercorn sauce, with duck breast, 95

New wave niçoise, 33, 42
Niçoise olives, about, 12
Noodle & vegetable salad, Asian, with ginger dressing, 52
Northern Italian bean salad, 50
Nut torte, dark & white chocolate, 143, 146
Nut, macadamia, coconut cookies, 148
Nuts, about, 12

Olive-basil bread, 58
Olives, herbed, José's 15
Onions, caramelized & roasted chestnuts, with veal
    chops, 98
Orecchiette with sun-dried tomato pesto, 68
Oriental dressing, 41
Osso buco, 97
Oven fries, with Caren's pepper steak, 100, 105

Pacific coast halibut cheeks, 111
Pancetta, about, 12
Papaya-avocado salsa, with crab cakes, 24, 36
Parmesan-prosciutto fingers, 20
PASTAS
    Asian pasta with black sesame seeds, 64, 69
    Asian vegetable and noodle salad, 52
    Caren's pasta primavera, 66
    Cold duck pasta salad, 53
    Farfalle with Italian sausage and radicchio, 75
    Gnocchi with classic Italian sauce, 78
    Orecchiette with sun-dried tomato pesto, 68
    Pasta, about, 12
    Penne puttanesca, 67
    Prawns & caperberries, 120
    Shrimp-filled wonton ravioli with saffron sauce, 70, 74
    Shrimp wonton soup, 32
    Smoked salmon with black pasta, 72, 73
    Tortellini and chorizo soup, 39
    Wild mushroom pasta, 65
Pear & mascarpone cheese tart, 128, 141
Pecan, Georgia, cookies, 150
Penne puttanesca, 67
Pepper steak, Caren's, with oven fries, 100, 105
Peppercorn, green, & mustard sauce, with duck breast, 95
PESTOS AND SALSAS, see also: Sauces
    Avocado-papaya salsa, with west coast crab cakes, 24, 36
    Black bean salsa with quesadillas, 21
    Herbed tomato relish, with grilled fish, 110
    Sun-dried tomato pesto, with orecchiette, 68
    Tapénade, with tuna fillet, 112
    Tomatillo salsa, with blue cornmeal chicken, 88, 108
    Tropical salsa, with roasted chicken salad, 54
Phyllo & flowers, 131
Phyllo, apple strudel in, 140
Pine nut & Gorgonzola pizza, 61
Pine nuts, about, 12
Piri piri pepper, about, 12
Pistachio cream, with angel cake, 138
Pistachios & white chocolate, with butter cookies, 151
Pizza, fresh artichoke, 60, 71
Pizza, Gorgonzola & pine nut, 61
Pizza, roasted chicken with Brie, 63
Plum tart, fresh west Coast, 133
Poached salmon with spinach & vermouth sauce, 107, 114
Polenta, creamy, 81
Polenta, grilled, with summer ratatouille, 82
Pork & cashew stir-fry, 109
Portuguese-style chicken, baked, 91
Prawns, black bean, 118
Prawns with caperberries, 120
Primavera, pasta, 66
Prosciutto-Parmesan fingers, 20
Provençal, chicken, with wild mushrooms, 90
Provençal seafood soup, 31
Pumpkin soup, fresh, with toasted hazelnuts, 40
Puttenesca, penne, 67

Quesadillas with black bean salsa, 21
Quail, grilled, with sun-dried cherries, 94

Radicchio, about, 12
Radicchio & Italian sausage, with farfalle, 75
Raspberry sorbet, 125, 142
Ratatouille, summer, with grilled polenta, 82
Ravioli, wonton, shrimp-filled with saffron sauce, 70, 74
Red pepper sauce, with grilled scallops & corn cakes, 2
Relish, herbed tomato, with grilled fish, 110
Rice & black bean salad with ancho chili dressing, 51
Rice vinegar, about, 12
Rice, wild, with sultana raisins & shiitake mushrooms, 85
Risotto croquettes, 84
Risotto with fennel, 83
Roasted chicken lasagna with wild mushrooms, 80
Roasted chicken salad with tropical salsa, 54
Roasted chicken with Brie pizza, 62
Roasted garlic & shiitake mushrooms, with leg of lamb, 103
Roasted garlic dressing, with crisp iceberg, 48
Rolled Italian beef roast with artichokes, 101
Rosemary skewers, with marinated lamb, 26

Saffron, about, 11
Saffron sauce, with shrimp-filled wonton ravioli, 70, 74
SALADS AND DRESSINGS
    Asian vegetable & noodle salad with ginger dressing, 52
    Beets & chèvre on mixed greens, with champagne vinegar dressing, 34, 45
    Caesar salad with herbed garlic croutons, 43
    Celery root salad with mustard, rice wine vinegar dressing, 44
    Cold duck pasta salad, 53
    Creamy garlic dressing, 41
    Cress, apple & endive salad with champagne vinegar walnut oil dressing, 49
    Crisp iceberg with roasted garlic dressing, 48
    Field greens with Asian dressing, 41
    New wave niçoise, 33, 42
    Northern Italian bean salad, 50
    Rice & black bean salad with ancho chili dressing, 51
    Roasted chicken salad with tropical salsa, 54
Salmon fillet, marinated, with ginger, 115
Salmon, poached, with spinach & vermouth sauce, 107, 114
Salmon, smoked, with black pasta, 72, 73
SALSAS, see Pestos and Salsas
Santa Fe chicken, 25
Satay, chicken, 27
SAUCES, see also Pestos and Salsas
    Béchamel, in roasted chicken lasagna with wild mushrooms, 80
    Black bean sauce, with prawns, 118
    Classic Italian sauce, with gnocchi, 78
    Demi-glace, with veal scallops, 96
    Fish sauce, about, 11
    Green peppercorn & mustard sauce, with duck breast, 95
    Indian curry sauce, with lamb, 102
    Puttanesca sauce, with penne, 67
    Primavera sauce, with penne, 66
    Red pepper sauce, with grilled scallops & corn cakes, 23
    Roasted banana sauce, with Mexican chocolate cake, 127
    Saffron sauce, with shrimp-filled wonton ravioli, 70, 74
    Satay sauce, with chicken, 27
    Spinach & vermouth sauce, with poached salmon, 107, 114

Soy sauce, about, 13
Tonnato sauce, with turkey, 93
Sausage, Italian, & radicchio, with farfalle, 75
Scallops, grilled Asian, 117
Scallops, grilled, & corn cakes with red pepper sauce, 23
SEAFOOD, see Fish and Shellfish
Sea bass, fresh, with shallots, chives & cream, 113
Sea salt, about, 13
Seafood soup, Provençal, 31
Sesame, ginger chicken burgers, 89
Sesame oil, about, 13
Sesame seeds, black, about, 8
Sesame seeds, black, with Asian pasta, 64, 69
Shiitake mushrooms & roasted garlic, with leg of lamb, 103
Shiitake mushrooms & sultana raisins, with wild rice, 85
Shrimp-filled wonton ravioli with saffron sauce, 70, 74
Shrimp wonton soup, 32
Shuckers fried squid, 121
Smoked salmon, with black pasta, 73
Sorbet, kiwi, 124, 142
Sorbet, mango, 125, 142
Sorbet, raspberry, 125, 142
Soufflé, Grand Marnier, 134
Soufflé, hot chocolate, 127
Soufflé, iced lemon, 126
SOUPS
    Bloody gazpacho
    Celery & Stilton soup, 30
    Fresh pumpkin soup with toasted hazelnuts, 40
    Lentil & vegetable soup, 38
    Provençal seafood soup, 31
    Shrimp wonton soup, 32
    Spinach & fiddlehead soup, 29
    Tortellini & chorizo soup, 39
    Tuscan bean soup with tomato crostini, 35, 37
Southern-style beef, 99
Soy sauce, about, 13
Spinach & fiddlehead soup, 29
Spinach & vermouth sauce, with poached salmon, 107, 114
Spinach salad in bread bowls, 46
Squid, fried, Shuckers, 121
STARTERS, 14-54
Steak, Caren's pepper, with oven fries, 100, 105
Stilton & celery soup, 30
Stir-fry, pork & cashew, 109
Strudel, apple, in phyllo, 140
Sun-cured olives, about, 13
Sun-dried cherries, with grilled quail, 94
Sun-dried tomato bread, 57
Sun-dried tomato pesto, with orecchiette, 68

Tapénade, with tuna fillet, 112
TARTS
    Caren's apple flan, 132
    French frangipane tart, 129
    Fresh west coast plum tart, 133
    Pear & mascarpone cheese tart, 128, 141
    Lemon curd tartlets, 130, 144
Tomatillo salsa, with blue cornmeal chicken, 88, 108
Tomato crostini, with Tuscan bean soup, 35, 37
Tomato relish, herbed, with grilled fish, 110
Tomato, sun-dried, pesto with orecchiette, 68
Tonnato, turkey, 93
Torta, layered mascarpone, 17

Torte, nut, dark & white chocolate, 143, 146
Tortellini & chorizo soup, 39
Tropical salsa, with roasted chicken salad, 54
Tuna fillet with tapénade, 112
Turkey & turtle bean chili, 92
Turkey tonnato, 93
Tuscan bean soup with tomato crostini, 35, 37

Vanilla, about, 13
Veal chops with roasted chestnuts & caramelized onions, 98
Veal scallops with demi-glace, 96
Vegetable & lentil soup, 38
Vegetable & noodle salad, Asian, with ginger dressing, 52
Vegetable lasagna, hearty, 76
VEGETARIAN
    Asian pasta with black sesame seeds, 64
    Asian vegetable & noodle salad with ginger dressing, 52
    Beets & chévre on mixed greens, 45
    Bloody gazpacho, 28
    Blue corn fritters, 22
    Celery root salad, 44
    Classic focaccia, 56
    Cress, apple & endive salad, 49
    Crisp iceberg with roasted garlic dressing, 48
    Field greens with Asian dressing, 41
    Gorgonzola & pine nut pizza, 61
    Grilled zucchini rolls, 19
    Herbed cheese appetizers, 18
    José's herbed olives, 15
    Layered mascarpone torta, 17
    Mini calzone, 63
    Olive-basil bread, 58
    Orecchiette with sun-dried tomato pesto, 68
    Oven fries, 100
    Pasta primavera, 66
    Quesadillas with black bean salsa, 21
    Rice & black bean salad with ancho chili dressing, 51
    Roasted chestnuts and caramelized onions, 98
    Summer ratatouille, 82
    Sun-dried tomato bread, 57
    Warm chèvre spread with toasted baguette, 16
    Wild rice with sultana raisins & shiitake mushrooms, 85
Vermouth & spinach sauce, with poached salmon, 107, 114

Walnut oil, about, 13
Warm chèvre spread with toasted baguette, 16
Wasabi, about, 13
West coast crab cakes with avocado-papaya salsa, 24, 36
White & dark chocolate nut torte, 143, 146
White chocolate & pistachios, with butter cookies, 151
Wild mushrooms, with chicken provençal, 90
Wild mushrooms, with roasted chicken lasagna, 80
Wild rice, about, 13
Wild rice with sultana raisins & shiitake mushrooms, 85
Wonton ravioli, shrimp-filled, with saffron sauce, 70, 74
Wonton soup, shrimp, 32

Zucchini rolls, grilled, 19

# About the Author

Caren McSherry-Valagao - CCP

Established in 1978, Caren's Cooking School has influenced the food philosophies and techniques of over 10,000 people. Caren first started teaching cooking out of her home sharing the food and cooking experiences she collected while travelling the world as a flight attendant.

Her successful teaching methods and personal food style have evolved through her exposure to the world's renowned culinary establishments, including:

> ** Culinary Institute of America: New York*
>
> ** The Thai Cooking School: Oriental Hotel, Bangkok, Thailand*
>
> ** L'Academie de cuisine: Roland Mesnier, White House Pastry Chef*
>
> ** Japan Airlines First Class Kitchen: Tokyo, Japan*
>
> *(respected for its sophisticated presentations of Japanese food)*

Caren was one of the first Canadians to become a CCP (Certified Culinary Professional) by the International Association of Culinary Professionals. As an alumna, she continues to be active in this organization. As well, she co-founded the B.C. Chapter of Les Dames d'Escoffier, an international professional society that promotes the continued professionalism of women in the culinary industry.

Caren's ebullient teaching style has caught the attention of Canada's national media. Her knowledge and expertise has been profiled on:

> ** CBC Radio's "Gabereau Show"*
>
> ** UTV Vancouver Magazine - special pilot show*
>
> ** CBC-TV national program, "The Canadian Gardener" guest chef*

Caren's professional life is balanced by her commitment to her family of two children and her husband who shares her passion for fine food and wine.

Order Form

Most ingredients in the recipes are available at local specialty food or grocery stores. In some cases, I have referred to specific ingredients whose flavors I have found particularly wonderful in the recipes. If you are having difficulty finding an ingredient and/or are interested in using the specific ingredients which I use in the recipes, please send for a free copy of Great Culinary Adventures' Specialty Food Mail Order Catalogue containing a complete selection of fabulous foods at warehouse prices.

Vancouver Cooks with Caren McSherry makes an excellent gift for friends and family. To order additional copies please call (604) 255-5119 or complete the form and fax to (604) 253-1331.

❏ Please send me _____ copies of Vancouver Cooks with Caren McSherry at $22.50
❏ Please send me _____ copies of Great Culinary Adventures Specialty Food Mail Order Catalogue

Name: _____

Address: _____

City, Province, Postal Code: _____

GIFT FOR:

Name: _____

Address: _____

City, Province, Postal Code: _____

Gift Message from Caren: _____

❏ cheque or money order attached
❏ charge my VISA or MC

Card No.: _____

Exp. Date: _____

Signature: _____

Mail Orders to **GREAT CULINARY ADVENTURES INC.**, 1856 Pandora Street, Vancouver, B.C. V5L 1M5